Fox Pee

and

Other Remedies

Enjoy!

Marchiena Davis

Marchiena Davis

ISBN 978-1-63961-073-0 (paperback)
ISBN 978-1-63961-074-7 (digital)

Christian Faith Publishing
832 Park Avenue
Meadville, PA 16335
www.christianfaithpublishing.com

Printed in the United States of America

Contents

Critter Encounters

Dead Thing in the Backyard

Oh gawd! The stench was overpowering. Something is dead back there. I am talking about the "no man's land" that lies directly behind our fenced-in backyard pool. We own "no man's land," but I rarely venture back there because, honestly, that is not my department. My department is the interior of the house, except the garage, and the small fenced backyard that includes the swimming pool and the plantings in the limited space beyond the pool deck.

No man's land is wildlife heaven. It has tall grasses, privet, some plantings by my husband to try to tame or lay claim to the land and a whole lot of unidentified viciously-barbed weeds. I am allergic to poison ivy, so that is another grand excuse for ignoring the area.

Beatrix Potter would adore my backyard. I have a so-called "squirrel-proof" bird feeder that attracts all kinds of critters. I see numerous yellow finches, chickadees, wrens, cardinals, and the occasional bully blue jays. Under the feeder lie in wait the darling chipmunks that have not such a darling habit of tunneling. The squirrels run up and down the tree that holds the bird feeder that has yet to yield to their persistent attempts at raiding it. The feeder has a spring action that closes the little windows to the feeder if the weight upon the perch is more than feathery lightweights for which it is meant. It is rather fun to see the antics of the squirrels. They will leap upon the ringed perch and hang by their toenails, trying to figure out what went wrong. They will crawl to the top of the metal dome and chew away, hoping their teeth will create a gap to the goods. I have seen them successfully land on the perch and then roam in an endless circle, looking for access to the seed that has been shut behind a shield of metal. They finally leap off in disgust and, like possessed beings, try again and again and again.

The stench, oof, it was bad. My daughter-in-law was visiting with my two grands. We were happily splashing in the pool when a breeze carried the obnoxious gaseous odor past our noses. My nostrils flared. I did not say anything because I have a peculiarly sharp sense of smell, and others may not smell the same stuff that I do. The look on her face confirmed that the odor must be really bad. Our conversation led us to ponder what the source might be. We both decided it had to be rather large to have such a pungent punch. Could it be larger than a squirrel, like a dog? Had we noticed any lost dog posters? Then the breeze would settle down, and our conversation settled down with it. It picked back up with the next breeze, and we then tentatively voiced our silent concerns that maybe the dead thing was larger than a dog. Horrors!

I worked at a summer camp for five summers as crafts director. It was not the most rustic camp around since we had air-conditioning for the adults, but there were rustic aspects. Most of the winter critters made their annual exit when the camp began its "opening of camp" preparations. However, some stubbornly clung to their new abode. One mouse or rat, or whatever, died behind the walls of my bedroom. The odor was horrible. I put my sheet over my mouth and nostrils to stem the onslaught of decaying matter stink. I placed a work order for the maintenance man to locate and remove the offending body. He laughed his head off at me. I felt kind of stupid. His final words were "Just wait three days, and the smell will go away."

Based on that experience at camp, I knew that the backyard stench would go away after three days, or could it be longer with a larger carcass? After three days, my curiosity got the better of me. I donned long sleeves, long pants, socks, and shoes, and tentatively made my way through the giant weeds that had purple berries hanging pendulously from its boughs. I extracted myself from thorny limbs that latched on to me. The bees buzzed nervously around my head. The birds protested vehemently against my intrusion. I got more brave as I tromped down grasses that could slice my skin with an innocent brush of my naked hands and face. Perhaps the dead thing was nearer the creek, so I made my way to the creek side, scoping out the bank. Not a body in sight. Ah well, a mystery.

A couple of days later, I was sliding open the pool equipment closet door. I heard a thump and saw the motion of a critter that was trying to hide. Its six-inch-long hairless, scrawny tail gave away its location. Oh no, rats in the closet. I quietly closed the door and tiptoed away to the garage where the rat traps were kept.

Was it peanut butter you put in the rat trap or cheese? Cartoons usually use cheese, so I figured that was the truth. I rolled up a strip of Muenster and blobbed it into the well for bait. I had doubts that I could set the trap without it backfiring on me and breaking a finger or two. With my heart beating so loudly that I just knew the rat could hear it or smell my fear, I did manage to set the trap and place it between two buckets of chemicals near a copious quantity of droppings. I slid the door closed again, went inside, and started emailing my husband about the rat, the trap, and the cheese, wondering if cheese was the right bait. My answer was instant! I heard a loud snap, and forgive me, a *thump, thump, thump.* My hair stood up. Now I had to deal with a dead rat since my husband was not going to be home for three days!

But then, was it really dead? After all, the thumping was quite dramatic. I suppose dying like that is quite dramatic. I decided to think about it later and went on a morning run of errands.

The summer heat was going to be unforgiving regarding the rat and its demise. I emailed my husband. "What should I do with the rat?"

His answer was brilliant. "Get the shovel and shovel the rat and the trap together and take it to no man's land, as far away as possible."

"I can do this," I said aloud.

I found a shovel, a nice square-ended shovel instead of the rounded one. The more area at the front edge of the shovel meant the less likely the rat would roll off if I made a misstep through no man's land. It was a perfect rat shovel. I managed to scoop up the rat and trap together, trek out through the weeds, and stood on the edge of the creek, ready to give it a heave-ho to the other side when I figured I should save the trap. I let the rat slide off the shovel. I used the end of the shovel to push back the spring bar. The whole trap sprung away from the corpse and tumbled down on the lower bank of the creek, but not quite into the water since the grasses acted as a hammock for the trap. With that, I scooped up the rat, its body turned face up now. Beatrix, forgive me. The poor fellow had an expression of utter surprise on his face. Even dead, he was kind of cute. I made a mighty effort and flung the body to the other side of the creek, where it landed safely in an area that was downwind from the backyard pool. I hosed off the shovel and put it back in the garage. I washed my hands ten times after cleaning out the pool closet and hosing it down, poured disinfectant and more water to rid myself of the rat experience. Water is a wonderful thing.

P.S. I took the garbage out and found half of a squirrel tail beside the garbage can. Another mystery to solve, but for another day and another person.

Goat

━━━━━━━━━━━ ❦ ━━━━━━━━━━━

I feared those horns of the goat, the goat named Sissy. I could not tell if Sissy thought me her friend or foe. Usually when one sees livestock in the field, they seem restful, peaceful, and quite harmless. If they move, it is deliberately slow. Otherwise, they are either standing, cropping, and swishing or folded neatly on the ground, chewing, flicking, and twitching.

Sissy would not stay confined to her assigned fenced area, keeping company with the two camp llamas and two miniature horses. She defied boundaries and simply bent her front knees, at will, to drop beneath the aluminum railed gate that had a convenient dip in the center of the dirt lane beneath it. Only newcomers to the camp would be surprised to see a tan spotted goat chewing her way, inch by inch, across the field toward where her past experience taught her that people could be found.

This year, I was one of very few people to be found at camp since the time would be considered "pre-camp." A few adults were there to prepare the camp for the summer season. Sissy discovered me through observation. She could see that something unusual was going on at the crafts shelter. The screen door was wide open as I was hauling out all kinds of accumulated debris to be disposed. I propped the door open with an old wooden chair that was already split down the seat, and the veneer was curling up in a scroll. My mind and head were absorbed in the tasks at hand when I saw Sissy bobbing her head up and down with those horns getting uncomfortably close to me. She thought nothing of coming right into the room. Again, boundaries were invisible to her.

My only other encounter with a goat was quite unpleasant, so I was leery of this one too. A cow or a pony has that soft dewy look in their eyes and their coats are invitingly touchable. A goat, on the other hand, has horns that dominate its head and loom over eyes that are bulging out with more white showing than color. The coat looks as if it were made of wire, with straight whiskers under the chin. There is not a hint of a smile on those lips. This goat looked like it meant business, and I did not want to find out what kind. My idea of shooing the goat out of the craft shelter was to stand behind the closet door and say in very clear English, "Shoo! Shoo! Go away now." This did not impress Sissy in the least. My next strategy was to simply stand quietly in the closet with the door closed, hoping that Sissy would lose interest and turn around and exit to her outdoors. Occasionally, I would peek out to see if she had left. I was also curious about what she was doing. I had always heard that goats will eat anything, and my concern was that she was nibbling on paint brushes or polishing off a jar of Mod Podge. This was not the case. She simply stood there, motionless, with her bulgy eyes trained on the closet door, waiting for the next movement on my part. After some ten minutes and her not losing the slightest bit of interest in my actions, I was afraid that I would be barricaded in the supply closet with a goat as guard for the unforeseeable future. This was not going to work.

What could I do to regain my freedom? I tried flying out of the closet unexpectedly, letting out a loud shriek. This only intrigued her more. It also made me more nervous. In looking around the supply closet, I found a roll of vinyl flooring standing in the corner. Maybe I could use this six foot length to prod her out the door. I picked up the roll and held it out at arm's length and pointed it in Sissy's direction. She took one look at this peculiar object that was coming at her with tentative thrusts and turned her horns around, showed me her little flicker of a tail, and trotted on out of the crafts shelter. "Thank you, God, for providing me with a tool to get Sissy out of here," I whispered with relief. I learned to keep the screen door shut at all times from then on.

This incident did not discourage Sissy from keeping me company from a distance. After I told my tale to the groundskeeper of the camp, he warned me not to touch her horns because she did not like that at all. No problem there since I never had intended on touching any part of her.

In the days following, I would have an eerie feeling that someone was watching me. Sure enough, there was Sissy, observing me through the screen door. She would rub her face on the screen, occasionally letting a horn zipper across it. I felt as if I were in the fairy tale of "Billy Goats Gruff" each time she decided to trot up the wooden steps to the deck above the craft shelter level. I could hear her trip-trotting the perimeter of the deck. She left piles of pellets the size of oblong marbles to remind me that she was still there. Fortunately, her droppings were easily swept away, unlike herself.

My job was done by the week's end, and I would not see camp or Sissy for six weeks into the summer when I would return for a three-week stay to teach arts and crafts. At that time, I would see Sissy in the distance, noting that she was safe behind the fence. Occasionally, I would hear the reports over the walkie-talkies that were used to communicate between key people at camp, that Sissy was out again. Someone would leash her and lead her back to her own area. It wasn't the safety of the campers that they were concerned about. It was the safety of the flowers that were blooming so beautifully on the campus. Sissy enjoyed eating the heads of the flowers as much as we enjoyed eating dessert in the dining hall.

I believe she accepted the fact that she needed to remain with the other livestock until the night of the musical production. Now, the musical production is the highlight of the summer camp season. The campers and counselors work fervently to put on the production in just a three-week session. Elaborate props are painted, costumes are custom made, and the musical theater campers pull it all together for a one night curtain call for the rest of the camp and proud parents. As I was making my way to the open air theater, I saw Sissy, daringly close to the main camp. She was having dessert. I suppose she saw me and decided to keep me company on my trek across the lawn. This made me uneasy because I did not know if she was looking for revenge or simply company. The small band was playing a medley of the musical pieces with the notes floating our direction, drawing us closer with anticipation. Sissy got caught up in the festive atmosphere and started picking up her pace, leaving me behind. That was a small comfort to me although I saw that she was heading straight for the crowd of people milling about, waiting for curtain time. My apprehension grew as I could see that her intentions were not honorable. She intended on barging right through the crowd and causing a ruckus. My thoughts sprang about from "should I run after her and grab her by the horns?" to "how funny this is going to be," to "this is going to be terrible." The distance between the two of us grew as I contemplated what to do. Sissy was focused on trip-trotting right up the deck steps that led to the musical theater audience. I could see the co-owner of the camp mouth, "Oh no, there's Sissy." She shook her fist full of programs in anger. That caught the groundskeeper's eye; and with skill and dexterity, as easily as catching a fly ball, he grabbed her by the horn as she took her last charging step off the ramp. He yanked her away and trotted her across the field to confinement.

I was amazed. He had grabbed her by the horn and hauled her away, with no fear. I felt so foolish after all that I had gone through—hiding out in the closet, shooing Sissy away tentatively, and finally succeeding by arming myself with a rolled-up tube of flooring. All that time, it was fear that kept me at bay, not those horns or the bulging eyes. I shook my head and folded my arms across my chest.

"Hmmm," I murmured out loud. I watched her little tail flicker and grow smaller as she and her captor strode away.

Raccoon

"Carl, I have a job for you to do. There has been a raccoon wintering in that ceiling right there. You can smell it and see it. We need to clean all that up and trap the raccoon."

With that directive, my husband, Carl, being a parent volunteer readying the camp for summer, went about the task to rid the winter squatter.

Our sleeping quarters were right below the winter nesting place. The first night there, I had to pull the sheet above my nose to filter out the smell. I urged Carl to get serious about the raccoon and its removal. So he stood there under the plywood ceiling, planning the strategy, anticipating the rain of debris that would come down upon loosening the first corner of plywood. I was not there to witness the reveal, but I could tell by the straight line of his mouth and the new seriousness of his approach to the problem that it had not been pleasant. He was going to get that critter if it meant setting traps at every level of the building and at any possible remote entrance.

He was told by the grounds supervisor that the best bait was cat food, the fishy kind. With the cat food that smelled almost as bad as the raccoon litter, he set a humane trap in the region of the suspected entryway. This was at the junction of the roofline and the outside wall, just above the sleeping quarters. I pointed out to him an opening that looked like it had been chewed into a semicircle, larger than a mouse hole. A raccoon could squeeze through it if it had a mind to.

The next morning, Carl had successfully trapped a cat, logical since he used cat food. There are a number of semi-wild cats in the area, and the strong smell of fishy cat food would draw any number of them to that third level deck. Carl looked at the cat and was not sure if it was safe to put his hand near the trap door to release him. Upon further observation, however, the cat seemed a bit put out but not frantic or hissing or snarling in warning. So he took a chance and released the door and stepped out of the way. The cat walked out in a huff. Carl would try again.

Early the second morning, there was quite a commotion in the trap. Carl found a squirrel that seemed utterly astonished that he would be trapped with no means of escape. He was leaping from one wire side to the other and then from top to bottom, searching unsuccessfully for an opening. Carl believed the squirrel to be less of a threat than a feral cat, so he simply opened the door without realizing that the squirrel would leap as fast and far as physically possible. It went flying off the edge of the deck and three stories down to the basketball court. Carl's first reaction was "Oh no! The squirrel is a goner." Looking over the railing and down to the court, he saw the squirrel land, be still for a moment, shake himself, and then run like crazy to the woods nearby.

The raccoon must have been a keen observer of his fellow critters and saw that the cat food lure had its consequences, for the trap remained empty for several nights thereafter. In the meantime, Carl and another worker blocked that opening, replaced the damaged ceiling, and I was able to sleep easier. We all hoped that the raccoon had not been nailed into the interior ceiling in the meantime. Various folks reported raccoon sightings both inside and out. One evening, the counselors were having a workshop at a lower-level room; and about 10:00 p.m., someone spotted the raccoon poking his head through a dislodged ceiling tile, checking out the action. He did not stay long enough to disrupt the meeting. The director's wife was working very late one evening and stepped outside her office to stretch and look up at the sky. As she did so, she came face-to-face with our resident raccoon who was squatting on the edge of the patio, deciding what location to scavenge next. This was a welcome piece of information since now we knew that the raccoon was not trapped inside the building after all.

And now it was time to pack our bags and leave camp. Everyone had worked hard to ready the buildings and grounds for the campers arriving soon thereafter. Carl felt disappointed that the raccoon had eluded all his efforts to trap him.

The night before we were to head home, we decided to go into town for an ice cream cone. As we were driving along the main street, I looked down a side alley and saw what looked to me like a street festival in progress. We pulled into the public parking lot and were feeling that our last evening spent mingling with the townsfolk and enjoying the local entertainment would be one to remember. However, as we turned the corner to the festival location, people were dismantling tables, folding up chairs, and filling up boxes to load into their trucks. Well, I am not shy, so I went up to someone dressed in jeans, a plaid shirt, and a straw hat and asked, "What did we miss?" It turned out that late afternoon to early evening, the town was celebrating "hillbilly days." We had missed the whole thing—the singing, the food, the arts and crafts. Children were dressed in rustic garb, and folks were chatting with each other in groups. But the action was now over.

Instead of turning back to the car after assessing the situation, we decided to browse in a few stores that remained open. One store that carried cards, stuffed animals, and accessories was having a going-out-of-business sale, so my attention was drawn there immediately. We rummaged through the knickknacks and lifted a woven blanket or two decorated with teddy bears or hearts—nothing that we were interested in. Then I spotted a basket of small beanbag animals. Of all the animals that could be had, we found a raccoon at half price. He looked adorable as a stuffed animal. He came back to camp with us. The plan was to put him in the trap the next morning before breakfast, place the trap in front of the office, and wait to see if the director noticed that we had finally trapped the raccoon.

With a few big hints to him about checking out the trap and finally having him do so, we all had a good laugh about the camp raccoon and how clever he was to send a substitute to get us off his back.

Back at home, as we were unpacking our bags, I found the beanbag raccoon in Carl's bag. "I thought you were going to leave this with Warren as a gag." He just shrugged his shoulders and said, "Yeah, I thought about it."

Mouse in the House

The telltale signs of a mouse in the house were scattered about the laundry room floor. The smallest pooplets I have ever seen must be from the smallest mouse I will ever see. This led me to take a trip to Lowe's to find a solution to ridding my house of the mouse.

I visited Lowe's to find quite a selection of traps. Some snapped, some were glue traps, some were spinner traps, and then there were the humane traps. I chose the humane trap which was a rectangular tube on a tilt. When the mouse enters, following its nose to the blob of peanut butter at the end of the short tunnel, the trap tilts and the trap door mechanism releases with the shift of weight in the tube. I could see this from the illustrations on the cardboard; however, to make sure I understood the method, I dug in my bag for my reading glasses. I pondered the illustration and read the directions. I understood the process, so I made the purchase.

What was that snap sound? Did I catch the mouse so soon after setting it? Yes, indeed, the trap was in lockdown position. I picked up the trap, shook it a little, and felt no difference in weight. I knew that I must release the mouse, even in the dark of night. Where? The river greenway space seemed to make sense. The released mouse would have to cross the parking lot, the road, go up the street and down the street to find its way back. Was a quarter mile far away enough? I would take the chance. I drove my car with the closed trap in a plastic shopping bag in the passenger seat. I crept past the stores already closed for the night, past the storage units in the back parking lot. No one was around. I left my headlights on so I could see what I was doing. I didn't know how to release the mouse however. I opened the trap, but it would not stay open since the mouse was weighing down the end. I finally took a chance and used my fingers to prop it open, gave the tube a little shake, hoping the mouse would drop out. I saw a scrawny, hairless tail which confirmed the capture. It must have dug in to resist the fall. I left the trap propped open on its side and hoped the mouse would eventually put itself in reverse to exit the trap. I made myself a promise to come back in the morning to check the situation. As I headed back home, my headlights shone on some pizza store workers taking a smoke break at the back door. Hmmm, they probably thought I was doing something suspicious. Why was my heart racing? The next morning, I did return to the trap along the river path. It was empty, thank goodness. Hopefully the mouse didn't beat me back home because, in the meantime, I read online that you should release them three miles away!

The weather got colder, and the pooplets reappeared. I set the trap again and was successful again. This time, I decided to release the mouse at the other side of the bridge of the greenway, a bit farther from home and more streets and traffic obstacles to cross. I figured out that I could simply pull off the end cap where the peanut butter lure was. I wore leather gloves just in case the mouse was upset and wanted to take a little nip at my fingers. The leather gloves proved hard to use when pulling such a small tab on the end. I took a chance and pulled the cap off with my bare hands and shook out the mouse. It was as tiny as I thought it might be. This second mouse I could observe in the daylight. It sat there in stunned silence for a few moments, probably getting its beady eyes adjusted to the daylight, probably thinking to itself, *Where am I?* With urgency, I said, "Go!" and it obediently scurried off into the grass.

Three captured mice later, hopefully different ones, I got less concerned about how long to keep the mouse in the trap and did not feel the necessity to release it right away. I waited until 8:45 a.m. to drive the mouse over the bridge and to the greenway. As I pulled into the gravel lot, I saw a woman pulling two strollers out of her car. She had three children with her. I wondered who would push the second stroller.

I released the mouse, said "Go!" and off it went into the tall, tan, dried grasses. It scampered off past a painted rock. What was that? A painted rock? Did it mean something? Did a Boy Scout leave it as a project? I didn't touch it, but I did approach the lady with the two strollers and three kids and asked her about the painted rock. She confirmed that there is a painted rock activity in Franklin with its own Facebook page. The idea is to paint a stone, hide it, and when someone finds it, they report it on Facebook but also have to find another hiding place for it, sounds like fun.

The two little girls appeared to be about three and four, so I started a little conversation with them about releasing the mouse in the grass and how I saw a painted rock. I asked the lady, who turned out to be their nanny, if the girls could see if they could find the rock if I pointed them in the general direction of it. Success! The girls found the rock after playing the "you are getting hot/cold" game. I explained to the nanny that I was a former kindergarten teacher and couldn't help but to include the girls in the rock hunt.

The nanny suddenly looked excited, exclaiming that she needed a kindergarten/first-grade tutor for an afterschool program of which she was director. The present tutor was having a baby the very next day and would be out for five weeks. She hadn't been able to find anyone to cover for those weeks. Could I come today?

The timing was not my timing. The timing was something that was incredible to me, to be led to an opportunity that met my needs and that of the afterschool program director and the children. The day, the time of day, the purpose we both had while at the greenway, all these together proved a harmonious outcome.

I did ask who was going to push that other stroller. A friend of the nanny was meeting her there and seemed to be running a bit late. No, not late, just right. The timing was perfect.

Moth Prance

Any moths clinging to the exterior glass window, being drawn by the kitchen light, would peer in and say to themselves, "Ah yes, the human moth prance." Indeed, that is what I have been performing these last few evenings.

Anyone subjected to pantry moths naturally leaps into the prance. A moth flitters out of the pantry cabinet. The human being shoots out a hand into the air to capture the oblivious grey-caped insect. The first attempt at capture is usually futile, so the next step in the prance routine is to use your eyes and head in quick back-and-forth movement from moth to countertop while shuffling hands attempt to locate a suitable piece of junk mail to use as a swatting device, a prance prop. The eyes train on the flight of the flutterer, which by now is exploring its wide new world, aimlessly seeking a mate while exuding mating scent.

I find a piece of junk mail that has enough heft to make a difference and enough length to extend my appendage. I move my lips, forming mild cuss words that would offend no one and accomplish nothing except to increase my determination to crush that moth and its four hundred eggs. I stand still, swivel my head and eyes to detect that slight movement of a tiny moth flitting in the atmosphere, my arms akimbo, ready to dash hither and yon with junk mail flailing in the air. My crouched knees are ready to spring into action. I only accomplish a steady whoosh of air that enables the moth to enter new heights it had not considered. My prance routine does not end there. I walk purposefully with head turned upward, junk mail getting damp from sweaty palms, imitating the path of the moth, zigzagging around pieces of furniture, waiting and waiting for the moth to descend within my reach. There! I spring into action and swat, swat, swat, feverishly hoping that one swat will down the creature.

This is a nightmare revisited. One time, maybe a couple of years ago, I went in and out of the door that leads from house to garage, and a throng of moths accompanied me. I beat them back, but most would survive the gauntlet. They waited patiently, hovering at the door, hoping for a crack into my house. I was not too concerned about the moths since they were a nuisance more than a threat at the time. After a few days of beating back the moth mob, I decided it was time to investigate the source.

The garage is not my territory. Yes, I do have my yard shoes standing nearby along with my minor gardening tools. The rest of the garage is littered with cardboard boxes, plastic containers, pieces of manly construction equipment, plus the more serious yard tools. I peek into boxes and find that the contents look astonishingly the same. This is the prime example of the definition of the word *miscellaneous*. The variety of stuff ranges from small to large plastic things that I have seen before but do not know the purpose of, along with the recognizable screws, bolts, nails, nuts, wire, sandpaper, dust, grease, and an instruction booklet thrown in for good measure. Honestly, box after box with the same contents? Interesting, but no source of moth fodder.

I hit the jackpot when I opened the plastic-lidded bin reserved for birdseed. My exuberance in lifting the lid allowed a cloud of moths to rush up to my face. I backed up, fanned my face, and brushed bits of moth dust off my lips. Are my eyes deceiving me in the dimly lit garage? I drag the bin outdoors and see what appears to be writhing seed. Yes, the seed was in motion with larvae competing for food and space to knit their webbed home until time for the winged escape. I dump the seed for the birds and bats to feast upon.

You can imagine my panic when I saw a moth emerging from my food pantry! I was revisiting the vision of the writhing birdseed, wondering what contents of my pantry were alive. I shut the door and decided that if I saw more moths, a further investigation would be warranted; but at the moment, one moth was not enough evidence. Several more moths did make an appearance. I could put off the task of detection no longer. Each pantry item had to be examined for webs and larvae. I did this in a random manner, seeking out the grain products first. No sign of moth larvae.

The next step was to take everything out, remove and dispose of the shelf liners, and wipe down all the surfaces. My pantry is deep, which is nice for storage, but then again, not nice for storage because things are forgotten in the dark recesses of the cabinet. I pulled things out and expressed delight in long-forgotten items. I started looking at "best by" dates. What! A cocoon just under the lip of the spaghetti sauce lid? A larva, vibrating with motion while busily webbing, was found in the crease of a Ziploc bag. My trashcan was getting heavy, and I was not sure that the plastic bin liner could cope.

My flashlight became my new best friend. Its beam helped me find those larvae webs which led to moth cocoons.

I could easily wipe, squish, and dispose. Several moths were clinging to the underside of the shelves, mimicking miniature mummies.

I did some research on the internet and was relieved to find out that it was not a personal defect of mine to have pantry moths. They hitch a ride from the grocery store. I could put all my food into the freezer for eight days. I wondered why eight is the magic number. Where would I then put my frozen food?

How such a small creature has put chaos into my orderly life. I have pranced the moth prance, cursed abundantly, and have stubbed my toe while tracking an upward soaring moth. I am on moth red alert level. Any oblong gray or black item measuring 1/2 inch sets off inner alarm bells. I hesitate before opening the pantry door. However, I do have lovely new shelf paper and neatly organized shelves—that is, until the next pantry moth makes its debut.

Yellow Jackets

E dwin, my yard guy, warned me about yellow jackets residing in the front yard of my new house. I inherited Edwin, along with a yellow jacket underground nest. I could tell by the expression on his face as he warned me that he'd had a more intimate experience with the yellow jackets than he ever wanted or hoped for.

A couple of days later, I had my wheelbarrow full of dirt from the dirt pile located in far left-hand corner of the yard. I was happy with that pile of dirt, which I needed since the yard, both front and back were dotted with ankle-twisting holes disguised by zoysia grass that crept along, no holes defeating its journey. I surmised that the holes, which ran linearly in starts and fits, must have been the voids left from old tree roots that had rotted away. As I wobbled along from hole to hole with my wheelbarrow and shovel, I noticed out of the corner of my eye some activity, low to the ground. I discovered the yellow jacket territory that Edwin had so thoughtfully mentioned to me. In the back of my mind, I knew to maintain an awareness of this species of the wasp family. I gave that area wide berth. Now I needed to come up with a plan of action.

Many years ago, I listened to Walter Reeves' Saturday morning radio show on gardening. I met the famous Walter when he came to our school as a guest speaker for the newly formed 4-H Club that I assisted with. He was interesting and fun. I saw him at the post office several years later. I was standing behind him in line as he held a parcel. I was kind of suspicious that this was Walter, but to verify it before making a fool of myself, I took every opportunity to make furtive glances over his shoulder at the return name and address but was unsuccessful until he set the parcel down on the nearby counter that helped keep the line in order. Yup, it was Walter, and I had no idea that he lived so close by according to the address.

I screwed up the courage to ask him if he was Walter Reeves—which of course, I already knew. He seemed hesitant to admit his identity. I mentioned that he came to our 4-H club meeting. That made me legit, apparently, because even though we did not have much of a conversation, he seemed relieved that I was not a kook. In hindsight, I should have just left him alone.

On one of the radio broadcasts, the subject of yellow jackets came up. A caller suggested putting a clear bowl over the yellow jacket entry hole. That was supposed to trick them into exiting the hole as normal because they could still see the daylight but ended up being trapped and eventually starving. That bit of information stuck with me. I left my wheelbarrow and shovel and went inside to assess which clear Pyrex bowl would work for this particular need. I even looked online to see if there was more to be said about the clear bowl trick. The only thing I found was on Walter's website on which he asked people to post what their outcome was, using this method of ridding a yellow jacket nest. Enough positive feedback was available for me to give it a try.

My dilemma was how to get the bowl on top of the quarter-sized hole in the ground. I also wondered if I needed to put a stone or brick on top to help keep the bowl in contact with the ground and stop any escape routes. Step 1 was accomplished by carefully and slowly placing the bowl, then rapidly walking away. A guard yellow jacket spotted my retreating behind and zapped me through my blue jeans, right on the fattest part of my bum. That made me scurry in a hurry into the house. I retrieved the Stops the Sting tube that my brother Rick had given me years before. I hoped the tube contents was not dried up or the ingredient potency expired. I dabbed the spot with a greasy smear and slapped a Band-Aid on it. If this didn't stop the discomfort, I would try some other remedies such as a baking soda paste or a cucumber slice or a used tea bag. I had no idea how I would keep the cucumber slice or the tea bag attached to my backside, so I truly hoped my first aid attempt would work.

Curiosity got the better of me, so I parted the sheers at the front window to see if I could see the result of the clear bowl method. I needed to get closer. Risking further stings, I crept slowly toward the glass bowl but stopped in my tracks when I saw a cloud of confused yellow jackets, inside and out, doing their best to make sense of this barrier. It looked like chaos to me, so I kept my distance from those furious critters. I decided to wait until dusk to place the brick atop the bowl and to retrieve my wheelbarrow and shovel.

What I thought was dusk came. The yellow jackets were still in a tizzy. I looked online for the definition of *dusk*. Aha, it is actually well past sundown, and that night it was going to be at 9:22 p.m. I had no idea dusk was so close to bedtime!

I waited and successfully placed the brick on top and escaped detection this time.

The next morning, I was admiring the tenacity and energy that the yellow jackets continued to display, a frenzy of wasps hovering above the glass, and the inside of the bowl seemed to have enough pests crowding the glass that I could almost hear them screaming to be let out. I turned my back on them. I looked a few hours later. That's when I saw an escape tunnel leading under the glass rim. Okay, now for the sake of Edwin, I had to take a more serious approach.

I climbed into my car and drove over to the Homeowners Pest Control store not far away. I consulted with the owner of the store, and he gave me precise instructions on how to handle this swarm. I was to wait until dark, remove the bowl, squirt this potent poison into the hole, which meant I had to get really close since the little red straw was only about five inches long, and hope that I aimed correctly and adequately. Then I was to fill the hole with dirt, which I still had plenty of. My parting question was "What time of dark is dark?" He didn't even grin. He said, "Any time of dark."

I had plenty of time to think this through, knowing that dusk was around 9:22 p.m., so dark should not be too much later than that. I conjured up a safety plan. I planned to put my blue jeans on, wear my rubber rain boots with the pant legs tucked in, don my leather gloves, which I switched to my pink rubber gloves since I had to push down on the trigger of the can and the leather yard gloves were too thick to feel anything. The rubber gloves also had the added advantage of having long cuffs that would go over my winter coat. On top of my winter coat, I wore my raincoat since it would cover my poor bum, the raincoat being longer than the winter coat but skimpy on thickness. I put on my headlamp that kept settling down across my eyebrows, making it difficult to see well. I flipped my hood over my head and headed out.

I was armed with the spray can, a shovel, and a bucket of dirt. I pushed the bowl off and flipped it over with the shovel. I stepped back, trying to aim my head toward the hole to see if anything had spotted me. My headlamp maneuvers, tipping my head until it finally shone on the hole, showed there was absolutely no activity. It really must be dark! I scrunched my eyebrows, wiggled them up and down, trying to move the headlamp strap up. I tipped my head down to locate the hole, walked closer, sprayed several generous amounts of poison in the hole, stepped back to reassess—no activity. I dumped the bucket of dirt over the hole, tamped it down with the back of the shovel, and stepped back. With even more courage, I stomped on the dirt to really pack the dirt down. I gathered up my gear, peeled the sagging headlamp off my eyebrows, and took off my armor piece by piece. The Stops the Sting was wearing off, a reminder of who really had the last word.

Rules of the House

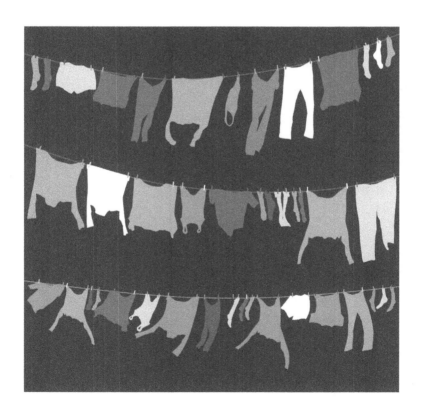

Fox Pee and Other Remedies

"Here, smell this."

"No way, no thanks, uhh uh!" was my response to my mother's demand to smell what was in the brown plastic wide-mouth bottle that she had dislodged from a makeshift hanger in a tree near one of her bird feeders.

However, my friend Laurie, knowing little about my mother, obediently took a whiff and nodded that she did indeed smell the contents.

I said, "What is it? Some kind of pee?"

Laurie looked at me in mild horror and more intense horror when my mom announced, "Yes, how did you know? It's fox pee. It's supposed to keep the squirrels away."

I said, "I knew it! No way was I going to smell that stuff."

Laurie gave me a quick "thanks a lot" look and turned to look politely interested as my mother continued, without pause, not aware of our exchange of looks. She was taking us on a tour of her garden that is an instant attraction to all new visitors. I tagged along and wondered how anyone could get that much pee out of a fox.

My first recollection of mistrusting my mother in this way began about twenty-five years ago when she served my husband and me a dinner that she vaguely mentioned was made with chicken. It was a nice noodle and chicken casserole that we all partook of, and I even had seconds. As we were sitting around the table enjoying a chat, she said to me, "Well, did you like the chicken?"

I was not even remotely suspicious of this question and answered, "Why, yes, thank you."

"It is rabbit" was her instant reply, with a gleefully triumphant look. I gagged, and my husband grimaced.

"Don't be so silly. You eat chicken, pork, and beef, so why not rabbit?"

"But was this one of the bunnies from the pen out there?"

"Sure, that's why your dad and I started raising them."

I gave a faint reply, something like, "I thought you were selling them, not eating them."

Since that time, I have not been able to eat any noodle casserole that looks remotely like the rabbit surprise casserole that my mom slyly served us. I began to look upon many of my mother's activities with wariness.

I think that the postman should have been suspicious of any packages that got delivered to Mom's doorstep. What if that fox pee had leaked out of its container? Mom would probably reply something about the mail being safe from squirrels and dismiss the whole idea with a wave of her hand. She had mail order worms and lady bugs delivered, each to be introduced to her garden. The fact is, Mom prefers to use unconventional methods to keep unwanted animals and creatures out of her garden.

Once she called me on the phone and asked if I would go to a dog-grooming place and ask for a bag of dog hair. She was without a car, which is unconventional in itself, so it fell upon me to say either "no way" or "okay." That time, I felt there was little harm in this mission and went equipped with a plastic bag. It did not occur to me that this was an unusual request until I made it. From the looks on the groomers' faces, I could tell that this was peculiar, but they went along with it. I believe they eagerly grasped this as fodder for a tall tale they could share. With a bag full of dog hair, I made good on my promise and delivered it to my mom. She was delighted and immediately started to sprinkle dog hair around the perimeter of her garden. The purpose? To keep cats at bay.

She has a love-hate relationship with squirrels. One moment she may be bellowing out the window at the squirrels raiding her bird feeders, and then the next, kindly putting out corn cobs for the very same rodents in another part of her garden. It upsets her that they don't comply with the parameters she has established for them. I asked her why she can't stand the squirrels. She said, "They eat the bird food, they dig up my bulbs, and they just make a mess!" *They just make a mess*, I thought to myself as I looked about her garden that was festooned with dog hair, plastic bottles hanging from trees, and paths that are covered with carpet remnants and newspaper for weed block. Imagine that!

Aphids are another headache for any gardener. Her remedy is to give them a blast from a sprayer bottle filled with some kind of murky-looking concoction. Seems to work as does the little jar tops scattered about, filled with beer for a "slug party."

I wouldn't be surprised if my mother doesn't go out regularly recruiting turtles and frogs to join her war against insects. She talks to her plants on a regular basis and most likely talks to the frogs and turtles and invites them back to her place. If that doesn't work, she drafts them.

One of the unique traits about my mom is that she can get other ordinary people, such as myself, involved in her garden shenanigans. It must be the look of determination on her wrinkled face, as well as the authoritative badge of age that she wears as a short, straight helmet of white hair. This aura is topped with the sureness of her step and drive of her mission. People do not know how to say "no" to someone who has a charming Dutch accent and a vivacity that takes one by surprise. They find themselves agreeing to enter into cahoots with her ideas.

The butcher at the meat counter has been wrangled into saving suet on a regular basis for her birds and giving it to her for free. The "China man," as she calls him, has been roped into saving all the plate scrapings from his restaurant into a large bucket for her to collect once a day for her birds. No car? No problem. She has her two-wheeled wire shopping cart with which she makes her rounds.

She had convinced the teenage boy down the street to distribute the scraps of egg rolls and rice, as well as corn mash for her birds, when she is out of town. I don't believe that my boys, her grandchildren, would have a thing to do with that mess. She was disappointed that he did not throw it out evenly the way she does. "He must not have been listening carefully when I gave him instructions," she surmises. "Maybe I shouldn't pay him as much as I had intended." He was probably overwhelmed by what he had gotten himself into, and frankly, I was impressed that he even showed up for instructions and made the effort to feed those birds. I don't have the courage to tell my mom that what she is feeding the birds is similar to junk food. She is not doing them any favors by giving them that stuff. She is convinced that they love it.

Dumpster diving is part of Mom's regular routine which provides free chips, crackers, and cookies for her winged buddies. If I did tell her and even presented the evidence from an authority figure on what not to feed birds, she simply would not believe me. The only evidence she needs is what she sees before her very eyes of birds in a feasting frenzy. One time I did tell her, in well-chosen words, that birds make their rounds all day long; and if they look down upon her yard and see nothing for once, then they will simply move along to the next stop. This was to try to convince her that it was okay to go out of town and not fret over her birds.

My sister, who lives in Holland, risked being arrested for smuggling on account of my mother. Mom requested some kind of special plant from Holland that would deter gophers. Fransje, my sister coming for a visit, carefully wrapped the woody stems in plastic and hid them amongst her personal items. That was a big risk on her part, but somehow, she was caught up in the plan and never understood how it happened. My mom's garden is ringed with these gopher-deterring plants that she has cultivated from cuttings of smuggled goods. The evidence is out in the open.

When Mom started composting, she somehow got all her neighbors to contribute to her compost tumbler. Most people usually conveniently dump peels down the disposal or in the garbage, but she convinced them to make special trips with their daily contributions, all the while scratching their heads as to why they were participating in this activity that was highly inconvenient. Mom has her way. Instructions were left to "give it a whirl after depositing peels."

I think I have figured out her secret. She approaches people with pure expectation and sureness that they will comply. A sharp nod of her head and the thin line of her mouth set in determination leaves people void of words to respond. They never know what hit them. I believe they benefit from this interaction with Mom however. They see the joy that her garden brings her, and it is quite a glorious "something to behold." Whatever stage of bloom it is in, her garden attracts life. Some of this life, she may not welcome; however, all are drawn with a sort of magnetic force to the simplicity and naturalness of this patch of ground teeming with activity. Her heart and soul, along with sweat and patience, are evidently expressed in her garden. Participants may feel a part of Mom's success as they move on the fringes of her activity. At first, they may have had a loss of words but soon find themselves caught up in newfound feelings and move slowly and methodically along with her routine, expecting to catch a whiff of her enthusiasm and nodding an acceptance of her unconventional ways. Squirrels, beware of Anna P. Boon's mission to convince you of your place in nature. She has her way.

How to Hang Clothes on a Clothesline

———— ✑ ————

M y niece, Melanie, visiting from Holland, needed to borrow my ironing board and iron. She told me that she does not own a dryer but generally can hang her washing so that it will dry fairly wrinkle free, but some things still need the touch of an iron. We talked about how we avoid ironing for as long as possible until we have enough to warrant wrangling the ironing board out of the closet. When we are finished with the task of ironing, we think to ourselves, "Well, that wasn't too bad."

I grew up with a multistrand clothesline in the backyard. We had a dryer, but to be thrifty, Mom used the dryer to get the worst of the wrinkles out, then carefully carried the tumbled clothes out to the clothesline to let the sun and wind finish the job. There is a method to hanging clothes on the line. Our mother made sure that we did it correctly and efficiently, avoiding gaps so every article of clothing could be squeezed in on the line.

There are rules. For instance, it is important to place the clothespin bag, designed to slide onto clotheslines, at the front of the line of wash, something that even a novice wash hanger finds out within seconds of beginning the task. Even better, wear a clothespin apron that has a large front pocket to hold the pins. Keep the basket of clothes at your feet within kicking distance. Kick the basket with enough oomph to move it but not tip it over.

Hang the socks at the toe to avoid a misshapen top. The toe can be hidden in the shoe. Hang matching socks side by side. You will have to save a spot for the mate, so move on down the line until the mate shows up.

Give each item a rapid additional wrinkle-releasing snap with a two-handed shake before pegging on the line. You will know you did it right when the snap and pop of the fabric is loud. A half-hearted snap of the fabric simply does not get the job done.

Hang shirts and undershirts upside down to prevent a clothesline crease across the shoulders. It is even more important to hang tank tops upside down to prevent unsightly humps in the middle of the shoulder seam or the imprint of the pinch of the clothespin.

To make sure you have enough clothespins by the time you arrive at the bottom of the basket, pinch one shirt corner onto the neighboring shirt corner, using one clothespin for each adjoining shirt. Are you understanding all this? The tricky part is to have nimble fingers to position the shirts, and at the same time squeeze the clothespin in place. You may have to hold the clothespin in your mouth temporarily, similar to a carpenter with nails.

Sheets: Make sure that they are hanging evenly on both sides and avoid letting them touch the grass. Tug at the corners to square them up. Make quick smoothing strokes over the sheets. Only use the cleanest of clean clothespins on white sheets.

Underwear: These unmentionables should be unseen, as well as unmentioned. Save a line between the other lines to hang underpants and bras so that they are hidden between the sheets or towels. We don't want the neighbors to view them while hanging or being hung.

One time, my mom shouted at me to bring the clothes in off the line since a thunderstorm was rumbling in the distance. I resented the idea of tackling sheets and socks while fighting the winds of the impending storm. Lightning flashed. I knew I had only minutes to yank everything off, throw it in the basket, and get it inside before the storm hit. As it turned out, my mother's fury was worse than the storm's. I had stuffed the sheets into the basket, grabbed socks off, making clothespins spin into the air, getting lost in the grass at my feet. She rushed out the screen door, the sound of the slam lost in the wind. She screamed at me for my thoughtlessness regarding the carefully hung clothes and linens, making a wrinkled mess of it all. I swiftly found out that rules for retrieving the laundry from the line were equally, if not more important, to abide by than the rules for hanging them in the first place. Wrinkles are easily crushed into the formerly smooth fabric with careless handling.

After being on the receiving end of those long moments of a tongue lashing, I wondered if the laundry was more important than my safety in an impending thunderstorm. Now as a mother myself, I understand being overwhelmed with seemingly endless laundry for a large family. A careless teenage girl can be the very reason for a rise in frustration and anger, especially when the time put into washing and hanging so methodically and carefully is undone in a few minutes' time. I knew I did wrong. I knew I created extra work. I knew I deserved that fit of fury.

Shall I tell you the rules on the proper way to iron?

What Are We Having for Supper?

———— ❦ ————

"What are we having for supper, Mum?" I asked.
"You'll find out soon enough. Now out of the kitchen!" was her usual response.

I was hungry and couldn't wait for supper to be served. My mom did not like us to be underfoot, but later, I found out that she wanted to keep tight control over the food in the kitchen. My dad gave her a very small budget for food and household items; so every morsel was accounted for, in her mind, for the next meal or snack. With five children to feed, it was a challenge to stretch the food so that everyone had a nutritious meal and there was no waste.

When I was six years old, it was my job to peel the potatoes. For seven people, that was at least fourteen potatoes, two for each. It was a hard job for me. My child hands could not grasp a large-sized potato in one hand and use the potato peeler in the other. The potatoes would grow slippery as the peel was cut away. I had to cut out the eyes in the potato before plopping the potato into a large pot of clean water. Because the potato skin had dirt from the ground on it, my freshly peeled potato was not creamy white but smeared with dirt transferred from my hands. The whole pot of potatoes had to be rinsed.

My mom taught me that the potatoes must be put in the pot of water so they would not discolor from exposure to the air. They had to be completely submerged.

"Try not to hold the potato against your shirt, Marchien! You are getting your shirt dirty," said Mum.

Yes, as I looked down, my shirt was getting potato dirt on it, but it was the only way I could hold the potato steady, pushing it against my shirt and chest as I made my way around the potato, peeling small strips of skin away and trying to avoid cutting my knuckles. All the while, my tongue in the corner of my lips, sliding back and forth, in concentration.

Another time, I asked, "What are we having for supper, Mum?"

"Ah, just in time to help me with the meatballs," she said.

My mouth started drooling. Large crusty meatballs, red cabbage with apples and cloves, and mashed potatoes were on the menu tonight. I was not shooed out of the kitchen this time. My mom had her hands up to her wrists in ground beef, squeezing it with her fingers to mix the salt, pepper, and bread crumbs before forming it into large meatballs. It was not sticking together right, so I was just in time to add additional dry bread crumbs to the mixture since her hands were covered with sticky meat.

"A little more, yes, hmmm, maybe a little more, yes, just right!" were her directions as I held the cardboard cylindrical bread crumb box upside down over the mixture, shaking a bit, then some more.

"Now to make the meatballs," said Mum.

She always had the same joke when it came to meat-balls. It was kind of gross, but she would say, "You know, the Italians use their armpits to make the meatballs. Shall I try?"

Of course, I always said, "No, no. That's gross!"

She would laugh at her little joke and continue gathering up a handful of ground beef mixture and forming spheres, ready to put into the melted butter in the heavy saucepan for browning. That was the trick to crusty meatballs. Brown them in butter, turning and turning until all the sides had met the bottom of the pan and were seared. Then add some water, put the lid on, and let them simmer, making a most delicious juice. At the end, Mum would lift the lid, pour off the juice, and crisp up the meatballs again. The meatballs would be moved onto a platter and the juice poured back into the pan. Mum would take a whisk and scrape the bottom of the pan to loosen the crusty meat and blend those bits into the juice. The juice was thickened slightly into a lovely brown gravy to put over the mashed potatoes. I could not wait for supper! The red cabbage was already simmering with the apples and cloves. The kitchen was filled with heavenly scents.

"Set the table, Marchien," said Mum.

We all sat together at the dining room table. My parents insisted that we eat together. It was a time to talk about our day, tell jokes, and be reminded of our manners.

Our dining table had two self-storing leaves in it. That meant I could pull out an extension by reaching under the short ends of the table, searching with my fingers for the handhold, tug, and pull the leaf out and up, then click it into place. At every meal, the leaves were pulled out and then stored back again.

Next, I had to put the table cloth on. I made sure it was even all around and straight as my mom taught me. I put the plates on the table first, one at each end for Daddy and Mum, then two on one side for my sisters, Fransje and Fenna. On the fourth side, I put three plates. My brother Rolf sat to my left, and Rick sat to my right, which meant I was stuck in the middle. I was the youngest, and that was the way it was. I gathered up the silverware, which was not really silver, but that is what we called it, a fork on the left side of the plate and the knife with the blade facing the plate on the right. Were we having pudding or ice cream for dessert? The dessert spoon was placed at the top of the plate. We used cloth napkins, so I looked at each napkin ring to see where each one went. We had a mixture of silver, plastic, and wooden napkin rings. Next, salt and pepper shakers were set in the middle of the table.

We always drank water with our meals. My mom said that milk was for babies, but later, I found out that she was trying to save money by having us drink water instead of milk. The glasses went on the table, along with a pitcher of water.

"Supper is ready!" called out Mum in her singsong voice.

My brothers came clunking down the steps, and my sisters put down their pencils from homework to join me and my parents for supper. My dad turned off Walter Cronkite on the TV and sat at the head of the table.

Under the watchful eyes of my mother, we passed the serving bowls around to help ourselves to the hot food. We knew she was watching so dared not pile on too many mashed potatoes or cabbage. The meatballs were easy, one for each of us and maybe an extra to cut up for seconds.

After supper, the boys and Daddy left their plates on the table. It never seemed fair to me that they could just get up and go. My sisters and I cleared the table, scraping the plates and stacking them to the right of my mom. She had already filled the sink with hot sudsy water and was stacking the dish rack with clean, hot-rinsed glasses. Glasses were the cleanest, so they were washed first. Then came the silverware, plates, and lastly, the pots and pans. My sisters and I dried the dishes and put them back in the cabinets. We were done in ten minutes.

"Rolf, come take the garbage out!" called Mum. He grudgingly took the plastic bag of trash to the outdoor can and relined the indoor can. Tomorrow it would be Rick's turn.

Back to homework and practicing music for the rest of the evening.

Thrift

Five children being born within five years during post-WWII Holland, proved challenging for my mom. My dad was unemployed along with thousands of other twenty-something-year-old men who survived the German occupation. She made do, with the help of some government assistance. Twice a week, we had meat on the table. The rest of the time, we had an egg as a meat substitute or just potatoes and cabbage. Desserts were infrequent, but usually it was rice pudding sweetened with raisins or Cream of Wheat with a bit of sugar and chilled so that it became congealed. She used a fish-shaped form for chilling the Cream of Wheat. When it was turned out onto a plate, the imprint of the fish mouth, eyeball, scales, fin, and tail were well-defined. We would fight over who got the head or the tail. Whoever got the body actually got a larger volume of pudding because the head and the tail were tapered.

Even though she led an affluent life growing up, Mom's common sense and practical nature kicked in to survive these difficult times. However, things did not really improve financially as time went on. My dad seemed to have itchy feet, so we moved from place to place, never really getting established. He wanted the American dream. He went to America after being recruited by a Pennsylvania textile company. After a year, we were reunited with him in this land of opportunity.

We didn't feel poor, but looking back and reflecting, I can see how my mom still had to make do with her tight budget. She set about sewing our clothes, giving us haircuts—which were embarrassingly evident in school pictures, and shopping for bargains at the grocery and thrift stores. We had potatoes almost every night. I remember too well since my chore was to peel the potatoes. What better food to fill our stomachs with than hearty potatoes—boiled, mashed, fried—potatoes no matter how they were prepared.

Our toys were few, but we took good care of them. We had mostly family board games, puzzles, or decks of cards. I had a pile of library books to get lost in. On rainy days, if we told Mom that we were bored, she would suggest we go sit on your thumb. That was a Dutch expression, and I still don't know what it means. Then there was the button box that Mom would hand over to us. One of my rainy-day pastimes was to dump all the buttons on the floor and sort them. Do you know how long that keeps a child busy? Should I sort by color, by the number of holes in the middle, or by size? Should I put them in piles or rows? My mom knew that would keep me quiet and occupied. As it turns out, sorting is a math skill employing attributes of objects.

The *Sears* catalog was a source of entertainment for all five children. I would circle all the toys that I wanted for Christmas. My brothers would huddle over the bra and girdle section of the catalog and swiftly shut it with a clap if someone came into the room. We knew what they were up to. Their faces told it all. Recently, my oldest sister admitted to looking at all the undergarments with great interest. She said it was fascinating. I am sure my brothers had another word for it.

Some pages had full-page-sized pictures of models in sweater sets or tailored suits. My mom showed us how to carefully tear out these fashion pages, pin them to a cushion, then use a needle to make needle holes close together, all around the edges of the beautiful model. The idea was to be able to punch out the figure and then glue it to some stiffer paper. I mostly remember my hand getting cramps or finding out, too late, that my holes were not close enough and almost impossible to punch out without tearing off an arm or a leg. My sisters were much more successful.

Another pastime was folding newspapers into hats, fans, or boats. We would set the boats to sail in the rain-swollen gutter or nearby creek. As a child, I knew all the steps to creating them; but as an adult, I am completely lost on how to replicate them, even after watching YouTube videos.

Between Parcheesi, Monopoly, card games, the button box, newspapers, and the *Sears* catalog, I would say that we had fun passing the time on a rainy day. On sunny or cloudy days, we were commanded to go outside and play. And play we did, with stones, sand, twigs, and leaves. We had plastic army men, cowboys, and Indians. We climbed trees, played tag and hide and go seek. By the time Mom called us in for dinner, we welcomed those potatoes and cabbage.

Tissues

─────── ⟳ ───────

M om and I took a few airplane trips together. It was challenging to travel with an elderly woman who had to stand in the security lines that looped back and forth for a mile or more in the Atlanta airport. This particular trip, I came up with a brilliant plan to accelerate the process. I knew when traveling with someone in a wheelchair, you could move right along through the line and even board first. Convincing Mom that she needed to be pushed around in a wheelchair was the difficulty. She was so dead honest that the idea of trying to deceive those in authority to jump to the head of the line was inconceivable to her.

I knew things were not going well when she, walking with a cane, me pulling our bags, heading for the elevator, suddenly lifted up her cane and hotfooted it over to the elevator door that someone was kindly holding open for us. *Oh dear*, I thought, the jig is up, five minutes into our journey! I wanted to hiss at her through clenched teeth, "Why did you do that? You need to act like you need a wheelchair!" I already knew that she would say, "Well, those people were holding the door open for us!" I knew my work was cut out for me.

Part of going through security is to have the carry-on luggage examined, either by an x-ray machine or a TSA agent. Since Mom's bag was bulging and could not zip properly, her bag got hand inspected. Off we went to a nearby counter for the inspection. She stood calmly by, but I could see that she watched with eagle eyes as each item was removed and laid out for the whole world to see. One particular item that she had in her bag made absolutely no sense to me. Apparently having a full box of Kleenex was of utmost importance to her. The TSA agent pulled out the box and rudely said, "Why in the world did you pack a whole box of Kleenex?" "I need it!" was her simple response. I took things into my own hands and smushed the box down so it would fit back in and zipped up the bag. She gasped as I crushed the box, but something had to be done! Apparently, to the TSA agent, a whole box of Kleenex is acceptable but not logical.

I managed to convince her to get in a wheelchair because the walk to the concourse was very long, yes, very long! That sprint to the elevator did drain her energy a bit, so she was willing to be pushed by a wheelchair pusher person as we went down, yet another elevator, to the train, and finally to the gate where we would be checked in. I made sure I parked Mom in the wheelchair as near to the gate as I could, keeping a close eye on her to prevent her from suddenly leaping up to use the bathroom or some such thing. Thankfully she didn't pull anymore stunts.

Her love affair with Kleenex has been ongoing. She made the most of one tissue, recycling it several times, blowing holes into it until it became useless. Between uses, she would stuff it up her sleeve, as we have all seen elderly people do. More recently, in the last months of her life, she would not only have a stash of tissues up her sleeve but also tucked inside a small lap pillow covered with a pillowcase that had a flap action to it in which she could slide the tissue into the recesses of the pillowcase, almost immediately forgetting that she had a stash growing in there. The pillowcase served another purpose. She slid her TV remote in the opposite end of the pillowcase, along with her timer. I couldn't fault her for finding multiple uses for her lap pillow.

When we had to move her to an assisted living place, I took her laundry home to wash since we had several incidents where an item of clothing never came back from the assisted living laundry or it took too long for the laundry to be returned. How many times did I have to learn the hard way to check her pockets and sleeves for tissues? Numerous times I opened the washer and found bits of paper covering every item. I had to shake everything out over the balcony of my deck as hard and furiously as I could to get major pieces off and hope the tiny shreds still clinging would get loosened in the dryer. I could only be mad at myself since I knew her habits good and well.

At one point, I took all the clothes that no longer fit her and took them home to wash so I could donate them to a charity shop. This time, I was smart enough to check pockets for tissues. When was the last time she wore this? How many years had the tissues been hiding in the pocket; and oh, by the way, it was always her left-hand pocket in which the tissues were stashed. By the time I pulled out all the compact balls of tissue, I had a plastic grocery bag full. I congratulated myself for checking the clothes because can you imagine what a huge mess of tissue shreds would have been found upon opening the washing machine once the cycle was complete? At least a whole box worth of Kleenex!

Gopher Delivery

Mom called me on the phone. It is always with urgency in her voice when she talks. Otherwise, an email was sufficient to take care of ordinary things. My heart always skipped a beat when I saw that the Caller ID showed her number. One time, she called because she was distressed that a $5,000 bed that she ordered was canceled because her credit was frozen. I was so grateful that her credit was frozen.

She had contacted the company that advertised this marvelous bed that had all kinds of features on it to make her rest and sleep guaranteed. She thought this would be the answer to her prayers since her sleep is interrupted with discomfort in her legs, arms, knees, back. The salesman showed up; and she reported that he spent two hours with her, and wasn't that marvelous?

I tried to explain to her in a variety of ways what it means to have your credit frozen and why it was frozen. With the threat of identity theft, I recommended years ago that she have her credit frozen because at age ninety, she would not be borrowing money for a house, a car, or any other large item for which she didn't already have the funds available. My explanations just would not sink in about the term *credit*, what it is, and how it can be frozen.

Nevertheless, we were both grateful that the bed was canceled, and her credit card credited with the down payment. A few days later, I drove to Franklin and took her to a local bed store and showed her a similar bed that had most of the touted features of the marvelous bed. Since it had an electric base, it was still costly but saved her $2,000 in the end. To this day, it is not solving all her sleep issues, but at least it is adjustable and has a vibrating feature.

Today's call was to report the astonishing delivery of two more "gopher" grabbers. I visited her a few weeks ago and took her two that I purchased at Target. These help her pick up things she has dropped or whack down things from up high. She likes to have one in each room. Two that she owns had lost their suction cups and were pretty useless without them. Before the visit, however, I found online that product for half the price of the ones at Target. I placed the order, but after returning to the website and viewing reviews, I realized that I had ordered a product that had bad reviews and people complaining about a waste of money. They broke easily, and the suction cups were not flexible, hence difficult to "pick things up." I put in a request to cancel the order and got an email honoring that request.

Today, however, with her urgent phone call saying that two more "gophers" were delivered made her upset because I might have paid for them without her knowing. I told her that the order was canceled; and I have no idea how they got delivered after all, and not only that, weeks after the expected delivery date. She stressed several times to let her know if I get charged for them, so she can pay me back. Her sense of indebtedness is supersized. She even tries to pay for my gas whenever I drive up to see her. If I send her something in the mail, she refunds my postage.

Oh, and she said that the packaging showed that it was straight from China. Sorry, China, I'm not going to send them back!

Clearing Out Bidwell

I fingered the needlework that I found in one of many drawers at my mom's house. It reminded me of all the projects with which she kept herself busy. She would take narrow needlepoint canvas and fill it with designs that were random, using leftover bits of yarn, taking color from one end to the other and ending up with a belt. She would affix eyelet holes at each end, the idea being to use a string of leather to tie the ends together. Each of us girls were gifted with these belts. I used mine to hold up my low-waisted, bell-bottomed blue jeans when they were in style in the '70s. It was a unique belt, but I was used to unique handmade items from my mom.

A friend from school would comment that I wore unusual clothes, but they were nice. My mom worked behind a sewing machine and made outfits for me without consulting me. However, since they were not hand-me-downs and actually suited me, I appreciated them. One was a dress made of brown and cream geometric linen fabric with a Nehru collar and long sleeves, like an elegant coat dress with buttons down the entire front, meaning many buttonholes and covered buttons. I came across one of those buttons in her old tin button box just the other day. I loved that dress. Another memorable outfit was an egg yolk yellow dress made from polyester knit (a new invention in fabric). The top had short sleeves and a scoop neck. The skirt was slightly gathered at the waist. It was comfortable and easy to wear. I felt cute in it in comparison to feeling elegant in the coat dress.

Now I moved onto another drawer. This one was filled with crocheted projects, partially finished. Under the crocheted items were knitted sleeves and other sections of good intentions to complete a sweater. Did she get bored? Did she try a new stitch and decide she didn't like it? Did she put it away until another day and get distracted with some more interesting yarn instead? She tried to teach me to crochet. All I managed to do was make a very long chain of single-crochet loops. She tried to show me how to knit. All I managed to do was make lopsided, varying-sized stitches, some loose, some too tight, in blocks of color. I had no patience with something that had to be done one tiny stitch at a time.

Many years later, my brother, recovering from cancer treatment, was gifted a knitted prayer blanket. The idea is that each stitch represented a prayer. The blanket wrapped around him meant he was wrapped up in prayers aplenty. He said he felt the prayers, the time put into each row, the skilled fingers making a blanket so meaningful and lovingly and purposely made to comfort the ill.

I remember coming home from elementary school, perhaps second grade, and catching my mom working on a lovely tot-sized winter coat that matched one that she made for me. She decided to confess, much to my surprise since I had no curiosity about it, that she was making some doll's clothes for my large doll that I received for my birthday that previous April. It was getting close to Christmas, so Mom took delight in making these clothes for my doll. I was disappointed that she confessed since I would have loved to be surprised by such an addition to my doll's skimpy wardrobe. I truly would have been surprised since I really did not give her sewing project a second thought. She could not lie to save her life, and if I asked about the little coat, she would have had to waiver between a lie and truth. To avoid being put into that position, I suppose she confessed before the question was even formulated.

What to do with these bags of leftover yarn, crochet hooks, and knitting needles of varying sizes? Unfortunately, any fabrics in her house reeked of mildew and were musty. Who knows what spores of mildew were being released into the air at that very moment? I stuffed it all into a plastic trash bag. My mom had not passed on, so I didn't feel the need to mentally ask forgiveness in case her frugal spirit was hovering about while I went through her boxes, bins, and drawers of fabric, yarn, papers, old towels, socks that had no shape left, shoes covered with a dusting of mildew, plastic magazine wrappers, all items in which she saw some potential for a future need.

Opening up cabinet doors revealed neatly lined up photo albums. These albums were filled with birthday, Christmas, Mother's Day cards, and thank you notes from grandchildren who received cash as birthday gifts. Mom used to get them government savings bonds but switched to cash at some point. I noticed that my niece, Caitlin, wrote many more thank you notes than my own children wrote. I could have done so many things much better than I did.

As I touched each item, made trips to Goodwill and Habitat for Humanity, put things for sale online, I thought how very difficult this would be if she was gone. As it was, she was just a few miles away at Franklin House, a nursing facility. Her house needed to be sold. She was practical about it and made suggestions to have a yard sale. I never had a yard sale of her items. I felt that would be so weird to haggle prices over household items, clothing, rugs, etc., and end up seeing her personal things walk away with someone who found pleasure in getting a bargain rather than walking away with a piece of my mom's ninety-five-year-old life. Instead, I dropped them off at the charity shops so I would not be the one to hand off the item for a bit of cash in return.

If the clear out of her house came after her death, each item I would pick up would make me feel sorrowful that she didn't complete that sweater or needlepoint or sewing project. Instead, I was able to pick up each item with wonder that she found time and patience to start so many projects, making do with what she had in the house, piecing together yarn bits, fabric scraps, and buttons into something unique, not requiring instructions or a pattern but her own mind and fingers, making something new.

Now her house is empty. I have in my home boxes and storage bins filled with very important papers as a record of her stages of life. Other bins have family items that I remember seeing as a child, things from her life in Holland, her time as a Japanese POW during WWII, family photos that only she knows how they are related to me. My sisters and brother have taken a box or two home with them. Maybe they will come again to sort through these bins and boxes, reconsider their importance, and hopefully take them so they are not hidden away in my home.

The weeks passed by, and I made hundreds of decisions on what to do with all of Mom's personal items. Some were precious, some were kitsch, many were from the local thrift store where she volunteered for years. I suppose she got first pick of the donations. I think the only things she bought at a retail store were food and underwear.

When I am ninety-five and have to clear out my house, who will take it upon themselves to sort through these papers, mementos, and understand the significance of that part of my life history, stretching back to my mom's life, things losing meaning over time and lack of family storytelling, lack of interest, lack of caring? I think of this often and hope that I will have the patience that my mom had to craft handmade items and be able to sort and label and even write stories to renew the significance of these material things. Then I will have done my best.

Mountain Scooter

The cashier at Lowe's was wearing a cast on her wrist. I made a comment to her that I didn't know they had a camouflage design for casts. She said it was hard to decide between all the choices. It reminded me of when my mom fell several years ago. It was evident that she had broken her wrist after experiencing a lot of pain and swelling. We took her for x-rays, and although the break was not severe, we were advised that she needed to have a cast to minimize any further damage and discomfort. At the age of eighty-eight, it seemed wise to secure the wrist since she was not quite as steady on her feet as she used to be. The dilemma came when she, in the midst of a wave of pain, had to decide on a cast color. It was too much for her, so I thought we should just go wild and crazy and choose a bright purple.

My mind went further back in time when at age seventy-eight, she broke her left arm just before we were going to a family reunion in Holland. I had no idea she had the fall until we met up in Holland, and there she was, with a sling and a cast on her left arm. I was so upset that she hadn't told me, but her reasoning was that I was on a prereunion excursion that I might have cancelled if I had known. She had to face a tricky operation on her arm that included a metal rod inserted to mend the fracture, without any family knowing.

The story goes that she was in her garden, working as was her passion, digging, rearranging plants, spreading mulch, weeding, all the things that I avoid at all costs. It was her custom to wear Dutch gardening clogs that had inflexible wooden soles. She said she wanted to take a shortcut alongside the house, so jumped off the little stone wall that divided her yard from a neighbor's yard. The wooden soles of her clogs made her slip off the wall and land on her arm.

I fussed at her and said, "Please don't jump off that wall again! It is too dangerous."

Her reply was "Next time, I won't wear my clogs."

Another incident involved her mountain scooter. This scooter had two speeds, turtle, and rabbit. Apparently, turtle was too slow for her, so she generally stayed at the breakneck speed of rabbit when traveling down Bidwell Street. The manager at Ingles told me once that he always held his breath when he saw her charging across Palmer Street on her scooter during the busy early morning traffic hours. For years, the thought crossed his mind that she would be hit by a car or be the cause of an accident.

I can imagine how refreshing it would be to go speeding along, feeling the fresh air on her face, the wind in her hair, and wearing a look of relaxed satisfaction, experiencing the sense of freedom that the scooter gave her to go about her business on her own terms. Her jaunts were usually short since the basket on her scooter was small, holding just enough food for a few days at a time.

In this incident, she was driving at rabbit speed down Bidwell but sensed a car was creeping just behind her. The driver probably was avoiding swerving out into the middle of the road to pass her. She saw her driveway up ahead, didn't slow down because she was trying to get off the road as soon as possible as a courtesy to the car driver, and took a sharp right turn onto her driveway, causing her scooter to flip over. The driver stopped to assist Mom and was extremely concerned that she had injuries. As it turned out, she had some road rash on her arm but was none the worse for wear. I am sure that the driver is still telling the tale of the little white-haired lady that drove her scooter down Bidwell at a reckless speed and still hasn't slowed down despite her scooter flipping over and scaring the bejesus out of him.

Once, a Franklin policeman stopped her, telling her that it was too dangerous for her to travel on the road. He told her to stay on the sidewalk. She asked him how in the world can she get on and off the sidewalk if it is not handicap accessible? She didn't use that term, but that is what she meant. He stood firm, so she decided to scooter on over to the nearby police station to argue her case to be able to travel on the edge of the road. The clerk in the office assured her that she was okay but to be careful. She never was stopped by the police after that or at least not that I know of.

After a history of falls involving calls to 911, trips to the emergency room, and finally landing in rehab for weeks, at the age of ninety-five, I had to do a role reversal and take her scooter keys away. When I told her, I made sure I was at arm's length. It was one of the hardest things I have ever done in my life, with the exception of whispering in her ear last week that it was okay to go. I told her I would be back in an hour. I voiced a rare "I love you." I left. She didn't wait.

Seeing a cast on someone else's wrist made my mind go in a direction that I hadn't explored for years. I am sure I will see memory joggers in the form of a garden flower, a jar of her favorite peanut butter, or a stick of ChapStick. When we gather together as a family, hopefully around her ninety-sixth birthday this coming October, we will share wonderful Mom stories, laugh as we hear things that we hadn't heard before but know they are true because that was what Mom was like—independent, quirky, but kind.

Parenthood

Road Trip Games

I reluctantly ejected the last of the six-tape audiobook. The story of Shoeless Joe brought us as far as Paducah, Kentucky, and we still had a couple of hundred miles to go. I turned to my teenage son and said, "You know, when I was a kid, tape decks were an option in a car, along with seat belts and air-conditioning. We didn't even have car seats for the little ones. I sat on my mom's lap; and my four brothers and sisters sat in the back seat, sitting alternated one forward, one back for more elbow room. We would draw imaginary lines on the vinyl seat as boundaries.

"Really? Well, what did you do for fun on a long trip?" he asked with a surprised lilt in his voice.

"We played games and sang songs. For instance, we played the alphabet game. We each had to find a letter of the alphabet on billboards and signs and whoever got to Z first won the game. See that A in Travel Lodge? That's my A, and now you have to find your own."

Michael got the hang of this game very quickly and was quite resourceful in using signs on the sides of trucks, billboards, and license plates. He zipped right along as I struggled with finding a Q. Of course, I had to keep my eye on the road while he was able to squirm around and spot the letters he needed on signs on the opposite side of the road. The mile marker posts were a reliable constant source for those four letters as we needed them. Then there was a lull when all Michael needed was that Z to win the game. Finally, being helpful and knowing I would never win, I pointed out a Z on a license plate. He said, "That's okay, Mom. I'll find my own." After a long pause, he volunteered, "Actually I saw about three other Zs before that one, but I didn't want to tell you."

Aww, I thought to myself, feeling a motherly warmth toward this son of ours.

I said, "Oh, go ahead and take it. I'll see how long it takes me to get to Z." In another ten minutes, I came in second place.

"You know what else we used to do to help pass the time?"

"What?"

"We sang songs. I remember one in particular that had verses that went with several instruments, the horn, the flute, the clarinet, the violin. I can't remember the rest. My brother would be assigned the horn. 'The horn, the horn, it wakes me at morn.' I got the violin. 'The violin's playing like lovely singing. The clarinet, the clarinet, goes doodle, doodle, doodle det.' We would sing it like a round. It was a lot of fun, you want to try?"

"No, that's okay, Mom."

"How about the cow game? You take a side of the road and count the cows, but when you go past a cemetery, you have to 'bury' the cows and start all over."

"I don't think so, Mom." By this time, I could see that he was starting to dig around in his backpack looking for his personal music gadget. I made one more stab at keeping his interest.

"Oh, okay. Well, another thing I used to do was to roll down the window and stick my head out a little and see how long I could keep my eyes open in the wind. Or we would stick our hands out and let them ride the wind. But of course, I wouldn't want you to do that! And also, we would try to get the truck drivers to pull their horns."

By this time, our son was hearing things about his mom that perhaps he did not want to know. I could see by the expression on his face and his raised eyebrows, the little shake of his head, that he was ready to tune me out and retreat to his own world. As he plugged into his music, I began to hum to myself, "The violin's playing like lovely singing." Or was it "the violin's ringing like lovely singing?"

Purple Hair

—— ❦ ——

M y oldest son has the most beautiful hair. His hair is the kind that people want to touch. His hair is shiny, thick, bouncy, and just plain healthy. I remember when he was about three years old, I kept his hair cut in a little Dutch boy hairstyle, framing his face in bangs and covering his ears in a blunt cut. When he would swing his hardest or ride his Big Wheel with intensity, that hair would simply flow in a shiny sheet of movement.

By the time he got into fifth grade, the popular hairstyle for boys was to have no hair, in other words, shaved. Well, the summers in Houston were intensely hot and humid, so that seemed like a reasonable style to sport. What we found was a short, brown stubble with white scalp showing through, with numerous bald areas due to scar tissue from boyhood mishaps with rocks or falls and cuts to the head. I was relieved when the hair grew out to a less harsh length.

Then came the high school years. I tell you, the girls were crazy about his hair. He once again wore his hair in a conservative cut and even insisted on going to Jay at Primo Hair Design to get the exact designer cut. Suddenly, the barber shop was unacceptable. Okay, so maybe we did take our chances at the barber shop. Sometimes the hair survived the barber's chair, sometimes it didn't. No more risks for this teen. His hair was so pretty that even the cafeteria workers at the high school wanted to feel it! How embarrassing for him.

Almost overnight, that boy decided to "express" himself. I thought, *Why not write a poem to express yourself? Why does it have to be the hair?* First it got shaved just around the perimeter of his head. As time passed, the perimeter of shaved area grew until there was just a strip of long lanky hair from the forehead to the nape of his neck. Throughout this progression, or rather, recession of hair, my son sported a top knot ponytail, braids, an artistic, symmetrical star shape shaved into the scalp, and finally dyed it blue. The girls still loved his hair. Go figure!

I believe the turning point came when as a swim team participant, he decided that the hair simply got in the way. That middle section of hair had gotten so long that it would stream under his swim cap and get caught up in his own wake. When tied up in a ponytail, the top of his swim cap made him look like a conehead.

I honestly never thought that I would take great delight in him shaving his entire head of all remnants of previous "dos." Things were pretty normal for about a year. He kept his head shaved. That actually enhanced his facial features since his face had taken on some manly angular edges.

Wouldn't you know though, the man-child got restless with the look. He came home one morning after going camping with some friends. I didn't notice anything peculiar about him since he was wearing a bowler type hat (another of his expressive styles since he liked Charlie Chaplin). But later as he was standing under the kitchen ceiling light, I yelped in surprise and pain. His hair was purple—no, more like magenta. "Chris, your hair is purple!" There was nothing else to say. I had put up with a lot of hair "stuff" over the years and kept my cool.

"Did you do this so you wouldn't have to go to church today? Oh, maybe your friends didn't have flashlights last night and they used your hair to light the way? And anyhow, how did the purple take so well on your dark hair? You bleached it first?"

It remained purple for a good long while. I called it his purple "haze." It was quite an attention getter which worked well where he worked. He worked at Eddie's Trick Shop. That was where people came to buy costumes, makeup, and hair dye, along with those cheap card tricks and gadgets. One night, we went to Toys "R" Us together as a family, and a little kid came up to Chris and said, "Hey, you work at Eddie's Trick Shop." A neon sign advertising for the shop? The Toys "R" Us cashier wanted to touch his hair. No matter what he did to his hair, people were just crazy about it!

Of Lamps and Shades

B^{*am!*} Curse those dogs!

Sierra, our sixty-five-pound Lab mix, and Skippy, the twenty-two-pound Shih Tzu, took it into their heads to charge around the crowded family room after each other. A detour under a glass and wood side table, with lamp atop, was easy for Skippy to negotiate; but Sierra, just a tail length behind and not aware of height and width of a table in relation to her already excited body, jolted the lamp right off with a hefty bam and onto the floor. This was a rare moment since Sierra was getting along in dog years and found it a groaning matter simply descending and ascending. Where this spurt of youthfulness came from was a mystery to me. The result of this short-lived romp together was a damaged lampshade to the one and only lamp that I had any attachment to. The dogs got a temporary reprieve when I found that the lamp itself was undamaged and still in working order.

Over the last few years of owning this lamp, I had given fierce warnings to the children about minding the lamp. They too would have spurts of romping about in the family room. Heaven knows why I would put something of meaning to me in that atmosphere. It was not a family piece. There was no sentimental meaning at all. However, the lamp marked the first grown-up purchase of a decorative item for our home. Although I had been a grown-up for quite a number of years—having husband, children, house, and dogs to prove it—this was grown-up in the way that it was not bought out of necessity or purchased at a discount store or acquired as a cast off but actually something that would be considered an indulgent purchase.

I spied the lamp in a real lamp store, was drawn to it by its shape, color, and texture. The base was scored into small squares, with each square painted one of four colors with a bit of gold on occasion, making it cheery in its uniqueness. The shade was nothing to get excited about except that it came with the base. This I did not realize was the exciting part until I went on a hunt to replace the dog-damaged shade.

Company was coming, and the shade looked glaringly shabby. My mission that day was to replace the lampshade and get new drinking glasses that were all the same size and free of that foggy look that water glasses get after a certain number of turns in the dishwasher. The glasses were found in a snap. The shade was a shocker. Not only are lampshades shockingly pricey, even at Walmart, but they come in a seemingly infinite number of sizes and configurations. The only thing about this mission that was clever on my part was bringing the old shade with me. My cleverness ended as soon as I casually tossed the old thing in the back of the car, not worrying about further damage or staining. Price tags soon gave me a new appreciation for the old well-worn thing that I had thoughtlessly clutched tightly in my free hand, further denting the plastic interior of the shade and adding wrinkles to the dusty pleated fabric exterior. At one point, I turned to a fellow shopper that I was vaguely aware of sharing the aisle with me.

I turned to her on impulse and asked her, "Do you think that this lampshade is missing the base for this price?" I showed her the $59.99 price tag. As soon as I completed my question, I asked myself, how in the world would this young girl, who didn't look any older than twenty-five, know anything about the price of lampshades? Surprisingly enough, she seemed quite knowledgeable about the price of lampshades and confidently told me that unfortunately, that is the price of lampshades nowadays. "Nowadays?" What was that supposed to mean? Did she look at me or my raggedy shade? Obviously, I was not up to speed on the price of lampshades.

That is when I realized that I had a new appreciation for my old lampshade that heretofore was not the exciting element of the original $60 purchase of the decorative, not utilitarian, table lamp. This time, on returning to the car, I opened the back door, half apologizing to the shade, and carefully placed it on the back seat before opening my own door to settle back into this mission. I decided a casual toss of the shade into the back seat from the driver's seat would not be acceptable. Now having new regard for the old thing, I decided that upon more careful examination of the shade, that a good dusting would be in order; and although the top half of the interior plastic had yellowed and the crack from the romp was there, I was not sure that our company would even be so observant of the little lamp that these flaws, so obvious to me, would be obvious to them. If I put the shade back on so that the crack would not be so glaring, maybe turn it to the back side, and put a lower wattage bulb in so the yellowing would not be so revealing of its age, I could get away with it.

One last possibility of fulfilling my mission was a home-decorating store that had so much stuff in it that you can't see anything or think because of all the distractions. Before wandering around in a daze, searching for the lamp-shade department, I cleverly asked a sales clerk if they even carried shades. Much to my relief and with hope in my heart, I was directed to the back of the store to a tall wall with various sizes and shapes of shades. I whooped in delight, temporarily leaving my shopping stupor, as I found the younger sister of my cracked, yellowed shade. What increased my delight was that it was only $19.99, and if I remembered correctly, I had a coupon somewhere in my purse for $5 off. What a day! I carried my purchase out to the car, opened the back door, carefully placed the new, white, sharply pleated, perky shade in the back seat, and casually tossed the old shade aside. Poor thing, its temporary reconsidered higher worth was short-lived and had now slipped back to its former demise due to a younger version of itself.

For Just a Moment

J ust as conditions are right for a flower to bloom, a butterfly to emerge, or a frog to come out of hibernation, conditions were right for a long forgotten feeling, a deeply buried experience that made me search beyond my immediate world.

I had a rare morning alone at home. Usually, such times are used as opportunities to tackle a project without interruption or read the whole newspaper instead of just the front page. This time, I simply plopped down on the couch in the living room and absorbed the silence. For a few minutes, I let my thought flit from one to the next, not resting on anything in particular. A thought rushed in, flooding out all others. I realized that we all spend our lives turning dials and keys, pushing buttons, and flipping switches to get our needs met. We have flipped, switched, and pushed our natural peacefulness right out the electronic door. With a pull, push, and a slam of the door, we have eliminated an opportunity to rest our body and resuscitate our peacefulness by the simple task of hanging wash on the clothesline. This takes more time to do; however, it is a time of renewal, a regeneration time. We are forced to slow our pace, think some thoughts brought to us by the cool breeze or heat of the sun, the rumble of the distant thunder, the flapping of a sheet or perhaps the retrieval of the clothespin that may have fallen from our mouth and led us to bend down to search the blades of grass and flick aside a grasshopper.

Sweeping the walk may add rhythm to our life and give us a reason to pause and notice the squirrel hesitating while on a food mission. Would a leaf blower afford us this same simple opportunity?

Washing dishes by hand forces us to examine that crack in the platter that we may otherwise not have noticed. It may make conditions just right to invite a family member to linger and visit during the final cleanup or allow us to secretly indulge in water play.

Bake those cookies from scratch instead of grabbing the Chips Ahoy! off the store shelf. What senses are aroused with purchased cookies, except the beep of the cash register, the crackle of paper, and the well-preserved crunch of the unexpired shelf food product, which blends in well with our time-efficient lifestyles? Otherwise, the senses we engage from home-baked goods are those of the warmth from the kitchen oven, smells of baked cookies, the taste of chewy, melted morsels, and the sense of the accomplishment of it all.

Are we healthier physically and mentally for all the electronics that control our lives? Those electronics have saved us so much time that we can squeeze in one more activity, one more life-enriching experience. They have afforded us the opportunity to become clock watchers for that all-important reality show.

Momentarily I sensed a new mission. Hang the wash, sweep the walk, grow a garden, take a walk, read a book, regain my mental and physical health the old-fashioned way!

Save those health club fees by doing what is natural. I became reenergized. My thoughts were racing. I had the answer.

Buzz! My inspiration left me as I ducked my head to shove clothes into the dryer, slam the door shut, and push the button. I heard a lawn mower start up in the distance. The neighbor's son revved his car engine, and the radio blared out and faded as the vehicle left the street, heading into the jungle of noise and electronics beyond.

Alas, my sigh was barely audible above the sudden clamor and din.

School Daze

My Foster Umbrella

Late in life, I returned to college to finish my degree. While the school was delightful, parking was quite a topic of complaint. It was not a problem for me because I looked at this as a nice way of getting in a bit of daily exercise by parking in a remote lot and walking ten or fifteen minutes to class. As the fall quarter marched on, I found that my daily walk became an experience that I could very well complain about. There were times that the rain would pour down in torrents, splashing back at my lower pant legs, soaking my shoes and socks and making my pants clutch my legs, my shoes grabbing hold of the wet socks, acting as fingers pulling the tops of my socks well below the heels of my shoes. If I stooped down to adjust the socks, my backside would get a soaking, and my bookbag gained a pound or two in water weight. My socks would lose total shape, being stretched desperately, leaving them heavily limp, exposing my ankles to the elements.

I realized during these moments that perhaps my young counterparts had something there—circling the parking lots for a prime spot, ready to pounce when any car looked ready to leave. A puff of condensed water vapor out of a tailpipe would be reason enough for a rush to that area. Or perhaps the sudden loud volume of a car radio that sprang into life with the turn of a key. My classmates had to have acute visual and auditory senses to be triumphant in securing a prime parking spot.

On one of these rain-soaked days, after making my adjustments to socks and shoes as best I could and listening to a professor drone on in terminology that I spelled phonetically so as to ask someone later what that was about (which was stressful enough, never mind being twenty-five years older than the average student), I discovered an umbrella under the desk in front of me. Before I could formulate a sentence to alert the student leaving the umbrella behind, she bounded out of the classroom, leaving me with a decision. Take it or leave it? I tucked the umbrella away in my book-bag to give to the owner at the next class meeting. The next class came, and the owner skipped that class. Okay, I'll just catch her at the next class time. I even wrote myself a note to remind myself to return the umbrella. I fretted at night, afraid that I would forget. So with note in one hand and umbrella in the other, I was relieved to see that my classmate had finally decided to attend the class.

With great relief, I presented the umbrella to my classmate, proud that I had remembered, proud that the umbrella was back with its rightful owner. I smiled, expecting profuse thank yous. The classmate simply looked at me and said, "That's not my umbrella."

I was bewildered. What had I done? The mother in me had become a foster parent to the umbrella until it could be returned. Although my intentions were impeccable, I had stolen the umbrella! What was I to do now? Was there a lost and found on campus? Two weeks passed. The window of opportunity for the owner to recover the umbrella at lost and found would surely be closed by now, wouldn't it? Another decision to be made. I tucked the umbrella into my bookbag and took it home.

When I got home, I took a good look at the foster umbrella. For the first time, I opened it to see the colors and design. Why, it was a lovely umbrella, one with a French floral design on it—sophisticated greens and reds—something that probably had been a gift or purchased by someone who liked it for its design rather than its price. My own umbrella was a practical black one, that any of my menfolk would not hesitate to use for themselves. I put my black umbrella back in the closet and kept the "French floral" in my bookbag or car. And I used it. I carried it with pleasure in the rain. It was a splash of color that everyone would appreciate. I took good care of my foster umbrella. When the fabric pulled away from the spokes, I carefully sewed it back on.

It did cross my mind that since I had another year and half on campus, someone would approach me in a downpour and remark directly to me something like, "Oh, I used to have an umbrella like that, but I misplaced it in class one day." I would gracefully, meekly surrender my floral glory to its rightful owner and slog on in the rain, pull my collar closer, or even hold my bookbag over my head as protection. Foster mothers would do that, you know. But instead, I carried my umbrella with a firm hand, striding about as if we belonged together. I had read somewhere that people walking with a purpose in their step would be unlikely targets of criminals. I assumed the same would work for me in this situation. I would simply walk with confidence in my step, snap my umbrella open with familiarity, and close it with a flourish. Who would approach me under those circumstances? No one has yet.

Housework or Homework?

I'm ironing. My household work needs to be done in one or two days a week rather than spreading it over seven the way I used to do it. I tell myself, "I'm ironing. I'm ironing. Don't think about homework." The mention of *homework* in my self-talk makes me think of homework and the list I have made for myself. "Okay, I have two days to get it done. It will get done, but now I'm ironing."

As a child, I was always apologizing to God for not thinking about him during silent prayer for even a few seconds. My mind would start with God but would wander through any number of other things after my fleeting thought about God. I'm ironing and wondering how those that meditate can do so for an hour while I can't concentrate being in the moment of ironing. What discipline! Good thing God doesn't stop thinking about me; otherwise, I would be up a creek without a paddle. At least I am thinking about God while I am ironing. That makes me feel better.

My ironing continues. I have used housework as a sort of therapy in the past. Whenever one of the boys would have a personal problem and I was still dwelling on it, I would start cleaning. By the time I had sorted out the problem in my head, I had a very clean house, mentally and physically.

Now the ironing is getting in the way of solving my problem. I am champing at the bit to get the homework done. Why am I making myself do the ironing first? I use my rational thinking and decide, while ironing, that to have the housework out of the way will make way for me to do the homework without the housework following me around in a thought cloud the way the homework is doing to me while I'm ironing. I have to decide. Do I scratch housework off my list first or the homework?

I stop my ironing because the rice is burning. I did that the last time I made rice, and what a dramatic mess that was. This time, it is not so bad. That makes me feel a little better that I am getting better at burning rice.

I am done with the ironing. I listen to Oprah's show on special fathers. It is the Friday before Father's Day. Although I am not a father, it inspires me to carry on with this journey of mine. At times, I think it sure would be easier just to stay home and lead a simple life. When I am leading that simple life, I am not happy that it is so simple.

Before I started this journey to be a teacher, I had a very quiet life. Because of that, whenever a repairman or a workman came to install something, I would anticipate their appointed time and greet them with enthusiasm, offer them water, and try to leave them alone to get the job done. When they were done, I would follow them out to their vehicle, asking them personal questions like how many kids do they have and how long have they been with the company etc. These were simply delay tactics so that I could have adult company for just a little while longer. They probably left me and thought, "She has a mighty clean house, but she needs a job, for God's sake!"

Yes, I needed a job outside the home. I needed one to keep myself out of trouble. Trouble like self-pity, restlessness, unhappiness, dissatisfaction. All the things that others long for, I had. I was not happy. My friends said that I was so capable in many areas that I could get a job easily. They were probably tired of me complaining about nothing also, and the job thing was echoing what the workmen in my life were thinking.

The Oprah program about selfless dads emphasized how they were making a difference in the lives of children. That is what I want to do—make a difference in the lives of children. That sounds like a commercial for an education program at a university. It sounds so trite. I need to press on to go through the hoops, do what the professors say so that I can get my hands on those youngsters and capture their attention and make a difference in their outlook on life and teach them math at the same time. I can do this. Others are doing it, why not me?

This is my job. I have hired myself out to Kennesaw State University for at least two years and maybe more. The income will be knowledge that I have to pay for with money and time and patience. I can do it. Stay in the moment, stop thinking about ironing and think about the goal. How long will this inspiration last? I must make it last. I have actual dreams at night that I am a teacher. I have a classroom of youngsters. I have order in the classroom and a pleasant, safe environment, and they look at me with respect and attention. They listen to me, and I listen to them. I pour my heart into the job, and my coworkers are saying, "Wow, she is sixty years old, and look at her go. She is an inspiration."

How self-indulgent is that? Well, after all, it is a dream, and dreams are not reality. I am smart enough to know that.

Realities Are Real!

"What! Where?" This is my reaction to finding out that there is a website that I need to visit often to retrieve and print my science labs, lecture notes, and grades. The same goes for my other classes.

I feel upset because they would not let me go to orientation to find out about these things—they being Kennesaw whoever. I am a readmit student. In other words, I have been to Kennesaw before, albeit ten years before. Kennesaw is a whole other animal now. There are new buildings, new places to park, new rules. I really could have used an orientation.

My science class neighbor had the professor's slideshow presentation printed nicely with six slides to a page.

I whispered to her, "Where did you get that?"

Her reply was "On WebCTVista."

"What? Where?"

No time for hand-holding, so at home, I gave myself a lesson on Vista, which some pronounce *Veesta*. Amazingly, I found it and found the slideshow. Fifty-three slides on fifty-three sheets of paper is not good. I had to solicit help from someone more computer savvy. The library has helpers for helpless people like me.

A week later, I realized that I was missing a section of the science lab. I thought I would have to go home to print it, but nope, *Veesta* can be accessed from the library. My nice neighbor said to "put money on my card." Oh, no, another piece of information I was missing. She could see my puzzlement.

"What card?" I whispered, hoping the professor would not catch me whispering in class.

"Your student ID card."

"You can put money on your ID card?"

"Yes."

"Wow!"

I go to the library and enter through the doors to the check-in and -out desk. I stand there momentarily. I must have had that perpetual look of perplexity on my face because the girl behind the counter came from behind the counter to lead me by the elbow to the machine where I can add money to my ID card. I was so grateful to her. I followed the very simple instructions and added money to my card. She stood by me to make sure that I did it right. Thank you, thank you. This was better than orientation.

Now I turned toward the bank of computers. I must be speaking with my body and saying, "Now what?" Another student in my class saw me standing like an uncertain child and came to my rescue. He showed me how to log on, print, use my card to take off money, and reminded me to log off.

"Oh, yes, of course, ahh, I see." These are my responses to wading through college computer land.

Hey, three weeks later, I was throwing my bookbag down on the floor, hiking myself up on the barstool in front of the computer, logging on, logging off, printing, searching. What a wonderful tool you are, my new friend, the computer.

Talk about being smart enough to do anything, I made a 69 on my first science exam. "Gosh, whoa, what happened?" I was asking myself. I laughed out loud at myself. This is reality. I left the exam all puffed up and thinking, *Hey, that was a very fair exam. I knew most of it. I think I made at least an 85.* Self-talk again. Okay, I will just have to do better on the next exam. Now that I have dropped that fourth class and my major science project is done and done, I will have more time to read, study, ask questions, see where I went wrong. Oh man, how embarrassing. Will I be able to face the prof? I can do this, jump through the hoops. Jump through the dang hoops! I am having to be my own coach through this. This is great practice for me as a teacher. I can empathize with the students. You know, I have to find some good out of this experience, and if it is empathy, I'll take it.

Even with my pep talk, I make a chart of my grades so far. They include lab grades, lab quiz grades, lecture quiz grades, project grades, and homework grades. They look pretty good except that dadgum 69 that stands out like a flag telling me that I need to do better than that, girl. It is a flag that says pay attention, stick with it. How can I be doing pretty well in all the other areas and do so poorly on an exam? I suppose I am not applying what I am learning.

I talked to my teacher friend, Jennifer. Thank you, Jennifer, for telling me that there is a solution to everything. If I do poorly in that class, the solution is to take it over again. It is not the end of the world. I don't anticipate doing so poorly that I have to take the class again, but it is comforting to know that it is not the end of the road for pursuing my goal. I do not have to find the nearest hole in the ground and hide until all the bad feeling goes away. I need to feel that bad feeling in the raw without the protection of a hole to hide in. It's okay. I can do this.

Ain't It Great to Be Crazy?

I am taking a music class. It teaches us how to incorporate music into our curriculum. What a fun time we have. I really enjoy the professor. Actually, she acts and talks just like my daughter-in-law. I get a big kick out of both of them.

So far, I have learned how to teach children a song through the rote method. I am no singer. I think I can sing, and I sing just fine around the house or in the car when I am by myself. In public, singing becomes another form of choking on words. My throat closes up. My voice sounds peepy and so soft that one would have to lean in to hear my whispered tune. I have to perform my lesson plan on Monday.

To prepare, I have jumped in the swimming pool and practiced my song while floating in the water. "Boom, boom, ain't it great to be crazy? Boom, boom, ain't it great to be crazy? Giddy and foolish the whole day through, boom, boom, ain't it great to be crazy?"

I know the words and the tune after singing it a half dozen times. That is about how long it takes a child to learn the words and tune, so I am keeping up pretty well with the children. Now I have to come up with some motions for the children to do while I am singing them the song as a solo. Sarcastically, I think, *Yahoo! I can't wait*. I have a plan that involves a *Cat in the Hat* hat. If I can be silly and crazy like the song, I can probably pull it off. That way, if my voice sounds crazy, it could actually seem planned. I am such a planner. I anticipate all kinds of problems and find the solutions. My problem is that I just can't sing, so I'll just sing crazy. That should fool everyone, right?

"Close your eyes, everyone." I put the *Cat in the Hat* hat on my head. "Okay, now open your eyes." My classmates should get a good giggle while I ask them if Mrs. Davis is wearing a normal hat or a *crazy* hat. From there on, I can take them through the motions for some of the words like "boom, boom" and "crazy." By the time they hear me singing the song three times, according to the rote song teaching guidelines, they will know most of the words. After all, 75 percent of the song is "boom, boom, ain't it great to be crazy!" I would be crazy myself if I chose a song with a lot of lines to teach through rote. I have a hard enough time memorizing the words and the tune. I needed all the help I could get. This "Boom Boom" song was the perfect match for me.

Laurie came over today for lunch and a swim. I added an extra piece of bacon to our BLT sandwiches and used plates with flowers on them since it was such a special occasion. She brought a bag of pretzels.

I thought about singing my song to her and going through the whole six-minute lesson plan but thought better of it. I didn't want her sympathy. She was already sorry that I made a 69 on my science exam. I told her about that, and she sounded just as disappointed and made all the right clucking sounds to try to comfort me. She is a great mom of four. She has two sons in college. She also has a young son in elementary school, so I believe I got a dual reaction from her. One reaction let me know she was disappointed and the other that things will be okay.

Since I got that much sympathy so far, I didn't think I could handle anymore. I might start to cry. So I decided not to practice on her. I would rather get the sympathy from my fellow students in the class. We are all in it together. Besides that, Laurie has a great voice and a musical talent. I wouldn't want her to throw up her BLT. We talked of other things such as family. We took turns lending an empathetic ear. It was quite refreshing to have her visit.

It was the day of my rote song lesson plan in front of the class. I went to the bathroom two times before class and one time during. My turn was next to the last of ten students. I was barely hanging in there and went through all the motions for the other lessons, and then it was my turn. I got all hot. My stomach was queasy. My hands were wet with perspiration.

I had the students close their eyes. I put the *Cat in the Hat* hat on my head. "Open your eyes," I said as planned.

They looked amused, but I had a feeling that my face didn't match the fun gesture of wearing a crazy hat. I was not relaxed and silly the way I had practiced. I was stiff with a crazy hat on my head. We went through the planned motions though I felt a little rushed. I think I added an unnecessary step, but heaven only knows. My saving grace was that my presentation was way more organized and smooth than the others, although rushed. I had my back to the professor so she could not see the expression on my face, that perpetual look of bewilderment that I carry on my face while I am on campus.

I got a kick out of some of the other students and their music presentations. When they forgot something, they would say out loud, "Oh, crap!" There was much giggling and "oh, wait a minute," stopping and starting and general confusion. My lesson had no colorful language and was stark compared to the antics of some. I hope I get a good grade for sticking with the plan.

Oh, how good life is! I got my graded lesson plan back from my music teacher. She had very few comments on it. That surprised me because I saw her scribbling furiously on everyone else's. The comments were simple and exactly what I needed to see. *Bravo! Great! Love the ending!* The greatest comment was "Hmm, there's just nothing I can say to improve on that!" Now was that not the perfect ending for a lesson plan?

Science Is a Science

〜⁂〜

Ah, fresh start for my science class. One crummy exam done and now on to new material. I printed off the PowerPoint presentation, and it looked pretty straightforward. Since many days had passed between receiving my grade and the next class, I went in without being too embarrassed. Apparently, the class average was 73, so I was below average, but not so miserably so that I couldn't lift my head out of the gutter. Besides, fresh start, right?

The lecture starts. The material is so foreign that my throat is closing in again. The last drop day is tomorrow. I will decide what to do at the end of the class. No matter what, I have to take this very class with the very same professor, so I decide that I will just have to *do it*! That sounds like a familiar refrain, something that I pulled out more than once for my college son. "Just do it!"

We learn that we can redeem ourselves by turning in all the homework assigned, correcting all the errors on the exam, and telling why the answer was wrong and why the right answer is right. The redemption is in the form of receiving one third of the erroneous difference. That could certainly raise my grade to a C, but why would I want to revisit that nightmare? Ugh, I don't even want to think about the process.

I got home from my 7:00 a.m.–8:30 p.m. day. I went straight for the freezer and pulled out the leftover ice cream cake from Father's Day. I helped myself to a hefty chunk. I think to myself, *This is going to make me feel better about my roller-coaster day. A hunk of ice cream cake will soothe my nerves.* With that piece finished, I dug into a pint of chocolate raspberry truffle ice cream that I got as a bonus for buying the cake. I ate half of that. Then I heard the garage door open and quickly shoved the pint box into the freezer. It was not cooperating and kept falling out. I knew I had just a fraction of a second before Carl opened the door. He could catch me in the act of hiding the evidence or if I was successful in finding a nook for the pint box in the freezer, I could get away with my secret method of indulging my mental hurts. If the ice cream had not been in the house, I would have found some kind of food to ease the bruised ego. The pint box was successfully jammed between the frozen waffle boxes. I was displayed nicely on the couch watching TV when Carl entered the scene. If he kissed me, he would know. If I didn't breathe on him, he would not know. I held my breath when he greeted me with a kiss, and I smiled with my lips closed.

Oh gosh, my stomach is hurting now. I had been so stable with my eating indulgences. My body was not used to this anymore. I am paying for it now. After feeling sorry for myself because my stomach hurt, I let my sorrow attach itself to my science class.

I made my way to Carl, tears in my eyes, and said, "I just don't know if this is the right thing for me to do."

97

He said, "Well, let me look at your science stuff, and maybe I can help."

My reaction was swift. I could feel rage welling up. I turned on my heel and yelled, "No! No! Five hours of science in one day is enough!" Poor guy, being yelled at for trying to be helpful. I took a shower. I went to bed. He came to bed later and tried to pat me on the shoulder and say everything will be all right. I started crying again. This is hard. I don't like hard.

In my math class, we had to do a group project presenting a math magazine article. I was in a panic this morning because the girl that put our paper together had it wrong, wrong, wrong. I called her and suggested that I organize the paper into sections that followed along with the article. She seemed to be fine with that, so I put the finishing touches on it and printed off five copies, one for each of us and one for the professor. It looked good.

I got to class early to meet my fellow group member, Allie, to go over our presentation. The other two girls could not get there early. She looked distressed. I found out that nothing was going right for her. Her computer had crashed. She was moving. She had too much to do for classes. Her asthma was being aggravated by the anxiety. However, she did feel like we were ready for the presentation, and we had gotten permission to present early in the lineup so that she could escape from class early to receive a delivery of a washer and dryer for the new apartment.

We did do well on the presentation. After we sat down, I noticed that Allie was taking deep breaths and closing her eyes; and every once in a while, I could see her eyes open ever so slightly, but not in a normal way. I ducked down beside her and touched her arm. She was startled by my presence.

I asked her if she was okay, nope, anxiety attack. She got up and left. After a few minutes I went to find her. She was outside, trying to get control of her breathing and her mind. When she saw me, she started crying. How well I know that feeling. I put my arms out to her and gave her a warm hug and held her. She needed to sit down. We went to the bathroom, and I talked her out of the anxiety attack.

"Allie, your brain is being held by this anxiety attack. You need to loosen the hold with a distracting thought. Think of Dr. Wilson in his underwear!" I was sure that vision of Dr. Wilson would detach that hold on her thought.

It worked. She chuckled. She calmed down. I helped her up off the floor, and I told her my story of having anxiety attacks and that she needs to find her strategy to shake it loose. She will, no doubt, face many more anxious moments.

I went back to the classroom and packed up her belongings and took them to her in the bathroom. She was so grateful. She went home. The last thing she said was that she had so many things on her plate. I said, "Yes, but you are scraping them off one by one until it is empty."

Gift Encounters

❧

I made a dash over to Bed Bath & Beyond to return an item. As I was getting back in my car and looking at my watch at the same time, a white-haired man was striding by. He had a youthful step, and his whole head smiled. *What an interesting man*, I thought as I saw that his pure white, long braid was finished off in a hand-carved ivory hair band that had an ivory pick woven in and out to hold the braid in place.

I had just enough time to get to my music class. That was not to be, since the interesting man came to a halt at the trunk of my car. He lifted up his arm limply and held his hand equally relaxed and said, "Oh, what a beautiful Volvo you have. What year is it?" Even his voice had a smile in it.

I said, "Well, it is going on ten years now. It is a 2000."

He was delighted for me. "My wife loves her Volvo. It is a 1998. Where do you take it for service?"

When he found out that I had no particular place to take it, he recommended an independent garage in Woodstock. That was the only place his wife took hers, and he completely trusted Doug, the mechanic. He proceeded to give me detailed directions on how to get there, but my mind was more on the time. Finally, I said that I was on my way to a six o'clock class, and I needed to head over to Kennesaw right away. He expressed his goodbye and started off. Just as I was closing the door, he ran back over and said, "Oh, we have two professor friends over there. Their names are…" It is here that I draw a blank on remembering the names. Actually, I did not even hear them the first time, never mind recalling what he said. I had no pencil or notebook paper at hand, so without that, I didn't have a chance of remembering names or phone numbers or exam times or scientific formulas.

I was speeding along to get to class. On the way, I was formulating my apology for getting there late and also conjuring up a description of this interesting man who wanted to have a conversation about my car. Now that I am recalling the encounter, it was actually touching. He was full of admiration for the qualities that the car represented. He had a love for his wife of many years. Seeing a Volvo probably meant he was seeing his wife in the shadow of it. His love for her expanded to the things she loved and treasured. What a loving, lighthearted man and interesting in character. He wanted to extend valuable information about servicing the car since after all, we had the Volvo in common with each other. He just oozed enthusiasm effortlessly.

I had my third meltdown in two days. That meant I was crying and complaining about the science class, again. I had a brain freeze over the material. I had an insane moment where I would just drop out of the program and become a substitute teacher at a day care or something. I even updated my resume and had a plan to drive to the five or six day-care places in the area and leave my resume. Maybe they don't take resumes at day-care places, but at least they would have my contact information.

I went to tell Carl of my new plan. His response was "You don't want to do that."

I said, "How do you know what I want?!" I cried again. I went to the computer to print off the next lecture notes for science class.

Miraculously, I made an A in that science class. The struggle made me a stronger person. The struggle to achieve anything is in the rearview mirror once we have arrived.

Lessons I Learned Teaching Kindergarten

———— ❧ ————

Things had settled down in my new position as a kindergarten teacher in a public school. I recently had one year in a private kindergarten class, but my field experiences had all been in diverse communities. I was ready for the challenge and was champing at the bit to make a difference in the lives of these children. What a trite statement, "making a difference in the lives of children." How often had I heard that at Kennesaw, but while in the field, I witnessed some teachers shouting at children to behave and get their work done. Could I make a difference?

My kindergarten team of teachers was composed of older women with many years of experience. Their approach to teaching was using a level head and a large dose of high expectations from the students. The work that these teachers were able to tease out of the students was amazing, far higher a level of work than I had ever seen. That in itself made my heart pound and my mouth dry. Could I, with so little experience, raise myself to their level of teaching?

Every day, I gripped the steering wheel of my car to drive the twenty miles along the back roads to my school. I would see people waiting at the bus stop, huddling in their overcoats at 6:00 a.m. I managed to avoid running over the early morning cyclers that were using their only way of getting to work. Once, while standing at a stoplight, a man pounded on my passenger side window, asking me to take him to a gas station for gas. That was his SUV on the side of the road. He had a gas can in his hand. I waved him off and said the light had changed.

My anxiety grew as I neared the school parking lot. Each morning, I felt as if I were scrambling to get organized for the day. I always arrived at school an hour before the children so I could get my materials together and go over my plans. Even the best laid plans were likely to go awry.

One morning, a young girl complained of a stomachache. She approached me several times about her stomach. Just as I told her to go to the bathroom and then get a sip of water, she vomited at my feet three times, in quick succession. The custodian was called, and the rest of us took a walk through the corridors of the school, trying to be quiet as mice so no one would notice us. That was the game, to sneak past doorways of the office, cafeteria, and gym. As we passed each window and doorway, my line of twenty kindergartners would duck low and tiptoe, trying not to giggle as we went by. A teacher walked past us and fell into the same formation, ducking by doorways. She whispered, "What are we doing?" I did not say that we were waiting for a copious amount of vomit to be cleaned up in the classroom. I just told her that we were sneaking around.

The honeymoon was soon over. The students with behavior problems showed their true selves. My anxiety grew. I lost weight. I cried and wanted to quit. Not only were the academic expectations growing, but the behavior issues were growing too. At times, there was blatant disrespect of the classroom rules. I found myself shouting. I would reflect on how disappointed I was in myself. My patience vanished as the fog does with the sun rising hot. I had a teacher observe the two students that gave me the most problems. He made suggestions, and I followed them. Things got worse. Weeks of frustration and unhappiness made us all anxious.

Then I found out, quite by accident, that a touch on the shoulder, a ruffle of the hair, a hand held gently was actually the answer. These children craved the touch of another caring person. I found that the touch of my hand, coupled with praise for doing a great job, whatever it was (and I found every tiny thing to praise) was the turning point in my relationship with the students and the turning point in their academic achievement.

On our last day of school, I only hoped that the life lessons I tried to teach them—such as be kind to one another or, boys, lift the seat before you pee or, help someone that has fallen down or, girls, don't tattle—will stay with them. I got a dear note from my brightest student. He said, "Thank you, Mrs. Davis, for doing fun things with us, not boring stuff. I love you. You are a good teacher." My heart melted.

My Stories

Our Chairs Are Gone!

─────── ⌘ ───────

S hirley, Connie, Elsa, and I go on our second "moms only" beach trip. Our baggage ranges from grocery bags to tote bags to the newest wheeled flight bags. Along with all the necessities, we each bring our personal beach chair, and I bring my watermelon slice beach umbrella. All this fits very neatly in the back of my minivan, especially with the third seat removed. Our snack bags are handy and the cooler positioned so that Connie or Elsa can just reach back to grab whatever cold drink is requested. The four of us are all set for our six-hour trip to the beach.

The trip always seems so much shorter with the four of us talking a mile a minute. Any little thing seems to set us off. Our foursome created a formula of cleverness and comedy that only gels under this circumstance. We are so "with it" and see humor in all of our experiences. We have a concentration of pure hilarity that none of us attains except when together for our annual trip to the beach. It is a feeling that I relish. The four of us must have some deep recess in our brains that sends special chemicals to the fore that make us an instinctively rare comedy act. It is unbelievably beautiful.

Our first step when we arrive at the condo is to settle our belongings in their places and head directly to the beach.

We are armed with sunblock, sunglasses, and our chairs and the one umbrella. With contented sighs, we set up our chairs to face the sun and surf, relishing the sea air and tangy salt spray. Each of us wears the broadest smile we own. Our gab time is nonstop. No subject is taboo. We make our stories about work, husbands, and children as colorful as possible without sounding ridiculous.

And how we love our chairs. Mine is the oldest, and I regret that it does not have the adjustable back that the other gals have on their chairs. I envy my friends when they can lean at various positions so that they get the benefit of the sun at all angles. They can avoid that white patch under the chin and the streaks of white where the folds of neck skin do not allow the sun to shine. What could be better than sitting on the beach with friends? What luxury.

Day 2, we arm ourselves with chairs and sun paraphernalia and hit the beach directly after breakfast. We wait as long as possible before heading in for lunch. Rather than dragging all of our equipment back to the condo, it seems to be safe to leave our chairs and umbrella sitting in our cozy semicircle on the beach. Other people leave their equipment out all day, we observe. After all, this is a family-friendly beach. With that decision made, off we go to lunch at our favorite fish sandwich place that is located at the back of a convenience store. Yes, you actually have to walk through the aisles, passing by the bags of chips and snacks, batteries and flashlights, and the sunblock selections. Then you walk past the public restrooms into a sunny sandwich shop that offers crab cakes, flounder, shrimp baskets, and sandwiches. The smell of fried fish is welcome to our nostrils. There is nothing like a fried fish basket with hush puppies and a bit of coleslaw to contrast the hot with cool and salty with sweet.

Lunch leads into viewing a video at the condo to avoid the hottest part of the day. None of us can understand the video; however, we stick with it, thinking that any time now, we will understand the point or plot and how the characters fit together. It never becomes clearer to any of us, and that's pretty bad because after all, we are the wittiest bunch on earth. This video is beyond each of us, and we make a stab at sharing the meaning of it. In the end, we just shrug our shoulders and say, "I don't know." With that movie still on our minds and our intellectual ability challenged, we head back to the beach to displace self-doubt with hilarious comments and observations on zillions of topics.

Shuffling along the boardwalk that takes us above the tangled shrubs, vines, and dwarf palm trees, along with whatever creepy-crawlies live in the dense thicket, we come to the top of the steps that lead down to the beach and could not believe our eyes. While we were watching that useless movie, someone, without family values, took our chairs! Man, we march straight down to the spot we had left our semicircle of chairs and lone umbrella and peer up and down the beach, trying to spot my very distinct watermelon slice beach umbrella, not a thing in sight that we recognize.

We are outraged and giggling at the same time. Can you believe that someone would take our things like that! And a family values beach, no less! I march to the right with some difficulty since that soft sand makes me walk as if I am wearing spiky heels, twisting and sinking at the same time. I head straight for a large group of people, and without even respecting their privacy, circle around them to inspect their chairs at close range. We go from cluster to cluster of people and chairs, finding similar chairs but faded, rusted, and missing parts such as arm rests or seat straps. It dawns on us that our chairs are really quite a find being whole and new, and my umbrella was the cutest one in town. With a big sigh, we realize that our original plan of sitting on the beach to watch the sun set is botched by a stupid movie and some bold thieves.

To salvage our evening on the beach, we sit on the built-in benches at the top of the boardwalk steps and eye-ball everyone and their chairs and umbrellas as they go by. Secretly, my plan is to stick out my legs to trip up the culprits and run with our belongings. Shirley keeps saying, "Honestly, can you believe this!" We cannot believe this. Making the best of the situation, we each imagine how the crime was committed. Each story is pretty unbelievable. For once, our wit is waning. To be thrown off kilter like this is just as much a loss as the actual physical loss. One serious suggestion is to place a sign on a stick at the scene of the crime to warn others. That suggestion is so lame that no one even bothers to remark on it.

Well, we cannot spend another day on the beach without chairs, so off we go to Winn-Dixie, eight miles away to see about new chairs, and of course, a new umbrella for me. Our evening plans are so goofed up by this breach of family values that we do not even bother to go out to eat, but rather eat English muffins and grapes for dinner instead. On our way to Winn-Dixie, we drop off that stupid video just to get it out of our lives. Upon arriving at the store, the four of us troop right to the beach stuff aisle. We see umbrellas, pails, bellyboards, but only three chairs. Oh no! One of us will not get a chair. Who will it be? We all think this, but do not say a word aloud. The chairs are pretty high up, so we can only reach them by prodding them off with my new umbrella. This is looking a bit dangerous since prodding may lead to chairs crash-landing. A nice teenage boy, not unlike my own, comes to the rescue. He says, "Ladies, follow me, and I will show you the rest of the chairs." This is a little more promising, so we obediently follow and are rewarded with the sight of about fifty chairs lined up over the eggs, cheese, and milk department. The young fellow is a good sport and hands down four chairs that we each point out to him. We "ooh" and "ahh" over how these are really nice chairs and even have a built in pocket that fastens with Velcro. We visualize ourselves settling into our new chairs with Velcro pockets, on the beach, each feeling a little better already.

This new chair is a big improvement over my old one but a step down for Shirley, Elsa, and Connie since these do not recline. But there is that back pocket fastened with Velcro! I say that we really need to try these chairs out to make sure they are comfortable, so we set up the chairs in the dairy department and sit in them a good while to make sure of our purchase. We are, once again, at our witty best, having recovered nicely from that jolt of reality, entertaining quite a few folks selecting eggs and milk. My husband and three boys would be mortified to see me sitting there in the dairy department of Winn-Dixie, in a beach chair, carrying on with my friends.

The decision is made. We'll take them. Anyone at all that listens to us gets to hear our story of how our chairs got swiped off a family values beach, of all things. These polite listeners look at us and remark how horrible that is and how could this happen at a family values beach. We really play it up and make our eyes big and shake our heads, looking down at our feet.

I think we are just as happy to get new chairs. I know I was. My replacement umbrella is bigger and better, and I now have a chair pocket. Eating bread and grapes for dinner probably offset the cost of the crime by at least 50 percent.

For the rest of our beach stay, we keep our eyes peeled for our beach chairs. I see one that looks just like mine, and I whoop out a shout and run to fetch it. One look shows me that it is not mine since it is missing the plastic arm rests. Even if it is mine with the missing arm rests, why would I want that old thing back? After all, who can beat a new beach chair with a built-in pocket that has a Velcro fastener?

Chimes

The wind chimes were dancing away in the slight breeze. The light aluminum pencil-thin dangles were delighted to dance their jig that increased in repetitions as the breeze grew stronger. They performed at the mere suggestion of a breeze. The chimes were driving me crazy. They reminded me of a dripping faucet or a pair of parakeets that didn't know when to be quiet or a gaggle of geese that answers each other with each one wanting the last word.

This was part of apartment life. I could live with the 2:00 a.m. coughing fits of my elderly neighbor below. I could ignore the regular chiming of the cuckoo clock. I knew these sounds were temporary and would stop in a reasonable amount of time. But the chimes were my nightmare as I tried to drift off to sleep each night. I would finally fall asleep, only to have the chimes incorporated into my dreams.

Although the apartment had air-conditioning and heat, my routine was to sleep with my bedroom window open to have some fresh air sweep over my face instead of the conditioned kind. Instead, the incessant rhythm of the high pitched chimes was sweeping into my bedroom. My thought was to nicely ask the neighbor to at least take the chimes down at nighttime. I then leaped to the conclusion that any excess noise that came from my apartment due to my teenage son and a resident stereo would have this neighbor rapping at my door in a nanosecond. What could I do besides slamming my bedroom window closed and sleeping with music in the background?

One night, as the chimes were at work, I decided to take some undercover action. I threw on my raincoat, took the broom, and planned to dislodge the chimes from their hook and let them rest on the ground as if the wind had had enough of them too. As a child, if I gave a thought to doing something against the rules, I was caught even before it came to pass. I was sure that I would be caught. Perhaps the scent of my fear would tip someone off. Perhaps the chimes themselves would protest so loudly that the owner would snap on the patio light and fling open the door, catching me with my broom midair at one o'clock in the morning. I chickened out.

A couple of weeks later, while trying to drift off to sleep with the chimes as my musical companions, I was plotting plan B. What could I do to rid my nights of the chimes? I could cut the strings they hung from. No, I really didn't want to vandalize my neighbor's property. I could wrap each aluminum dangle in bubble wrap—no, too time consuming, thus too risky. My mind searched each of my kitchen cupboards mentally for a solution. It chanced upon the thought of some clear packing tape. That's it! I could take a length of packing tape and just wrap those chimes up as if they were in a straight jacket. *Quick, easy, harmless*, I thought.

So that is exactly what I did. I took a length of sticky clear packing tape, hoping that it wouldn't fold over on itself between my second-story apartment and the patio apartment below. I prayed that no one would be coming up the steps or pulling into a parking spot with headlights beaming on me as I followed through on my ploy. I shook with fear. I plunged ahead with the plan despite the risks involved. I leaped from pavement to grass over a swath of pine straw that could easily give my location away under the crackle of my shoes. My tape was still sticky, my hands were too. I stood in front of those frolicking chimes. I muttered a goodbye to their cheerfulness. With tape stretched out between both my hands, allowing my coat to fall open to reveal my nightie, I quickly wrapped them up, the cluster of aluminum chimes finally silenced by the clear tape that saved my sanity. The deed was done. They hung huddled together in silence, still swaying in the wind but as a bundle rather than individuals.

My common sense kicked in, and I scurried back to my apartment. The headlights caught me coming around the corner. I hoped that the driver didn't see my face despite the dark. I couldn't get to sleep. My imagination kept me awake this time. I imagined the neighbor carrying the wrapped chimes from door to door and saying in an accusing manner, "Did you do this?" I know myself. I would tell the truth and ask forgiveness.

Nothing happened. The next morning, I gave a surreptitious glance in the direction of the patio chimes. The glance gave me no information as to the status of the chimes. I just let my ears be the judge. Each night I would open the window and hear the delightful sound of silence. This went on for a month. I finally got up the courage to walk as casually as possible by the patio. How could I look up in the direction of the chimes without giving away my purpose? I was getting better with practice at the undercover activity. Somehow I got away with it by pretending to drop something on the ground nearby and looking up in one flawless motion at the very spot of the chimes. I gasped. They were still wrapped up snugly, quietly waiting for a release. The owners hadn't even noticed. A sigh of relief escaped from my throat.

From then on, I could go about my business with a sense of freedom. I had gotten away with this petty crime. How could anyone find out the culprit? By now, I had practiced the confrontation scenario so many times in my head that I felt I could pull it off with a show of ignorance if I had to. Would those chimes ever dance again? They were gone the next time I looked. The neighbors probably wondered who, what, when. I know the answers, and they never will.

Porta-Potty Blue House

———— ❧ ————

I have a give-and-take relationship with the house two doors down. This began in October of 1995 when my family moved from one county in the Metro Atlanta area to another clear across town. When we put a contract on this two-story traditional home on a neighborhood lake, I did not note exactly what color the neighboring houses were. I know this because the houses were not screaming at me, "Look at me, I am bright yellow, or I am pink." They were, and still are, generally rather muted, earth tones that blend in nicely with the natural setting of mature trees and mild hills.

Closing day came, and we excitedly started moving our possessions to our new home that held so much promise. When driving into the neighborhood and turning left on to our street, my breath caught in my throat when I saw that every day, I would have to pass by the house two doors down that was now painted what we nicknamed immediately as "porta-potty blue." And what an apt description of that color, bold blue with white trim, just like you see on the johnny houses that are scattered about construction sites for workmen to use. I was so appalled by this turn of events that I drove right by our new home that is painted a blah beige with charcoal grey shutters and a lighter grey trim. All I could

119

think was how grateful I was that we did not live right beside this newly painted house.

My oldest son was at college when we selected our new home. It was a joke in the family that when he went off to college, we moved and forgot to tell him where. He did come home long enough to help with the move however. As a joke, I directed him to pull up to the porta-potty blue house.

I said to him, "Well, what do you think?"

He said back to me in a flash, "No way, Mom. This can't be it."

I laughed and said, "You're right, this is not it. Pull down two more houses."

"You really had me going there for a minute!" This gave us all a good laugh. But the house would not forgive me for that joke.

We pretty much got settled in before Halloween arrived. This neighborhood organized a hotdog cookout and costume parade, followed by trick-or-treating. Wouldn't that be a super way to introduce ourselves to the neighborhood? All went well until the trick-or-treating part. My nine-year-old son hooked up with two other boys of similar age, and we parents tagged along, enjoying the evening out and the camaraderie. Our adult conversation went the way of adults, exchanging information about where we worked and where we were from and so on. As we walked past the blue house, the words slipped out of my mouth without thought, and I said, "We call this the porta-potty blue house. I know it wasn't that color when we put a contract on our house."

This remark was met with silence. One of the dads in the group must have felt a bit of compassion for me and said, "I suppose it is a bit bright."

I was so embarrassed that I could think of nothing else to contribute to the conversation for the rest of the trek about the neighborhood, as we kept up with our trick-or-treaters. The word spread around the neighborhood, and naturally, someone had the pleasure of telling the homeowners my remark. I sensed when that happened because when I would walk or drive by the house, if the owners were outdoors, they would barely glance my way. So much for a new beginning. Our beginning had hardly begun before our reputation was established based on one thoughtless remark.

Five years later, I was able to demonstrate what I believe to be my true nature of caring and concern. As I drove into the neighborhood, past the blue house, I noted to myself that it was an awfully warm day to be having a fire in the fireplace. It also dawned on me that no one should be home this time of day, so how could there be a fire in the fireplace? Besides that, the smoke wasn't coming out of the chimney, but rather out from under the eaves. That house was on fire!

I called 911 and reported the fire. I said, "It's a por-ta-potty blue house." There I go again, blurting out that awful comment, and it being recorded by 911 dispatch. How humiliating. I could well imagine the dispatchers having a good chuckle amongst themselves with that remark.

I faithfully stood opposite the house so that when the fire trucks came, I could jump up and down and point excit-edly at the smoking house. I only hoped that the blue house was taking note of my redeeming actions. The fire was put out, the dog was rescued, and the homeowner notified by someone with more wits about them than me. The home-owner never thanked me for calling the fire department.

The house was stripped to the studs for renovation. A huge open dumpster was placed in the driveway, and a porta-potty was installed in the middle of the front yard for the construction crew. This one, however, was green and red, not the blue one that mimicked the house color so well.

"Blue house, are you doing okay?" I asked mentally as I went by.

One Wednesday, a lumber truck delivered its load in the front yard of the blue house. That night, as I was taking the garbage cans out for Thursday collection, a movement caught my eye. I turned my head toward the blue house and bent forward at the waist a bit to peer into the night to see what was going on down there. I saw two shadowy figures moving lumber. I saw a pickup truck in front of the house with the passenger side door open. My first conclusion was that someone was stealing the lumber! I thought that we had escaped that type of crime by moving to this part of town. Outraged, I started to trot on down there to see for myself if that was the case. I stopped myself, realizing that I may just get myself shot if I did such an impulsive thing. But someone was stealing the lumber. Well, I could pretend that I am going on an evening walk and assess the situation as I got closer. I took ten steps forward before I realized that I was wearing Birkenstock sandals and a red checkered apron. The pretense of going on an evening walk would not fly. The heck with it, I decided to go anyway.

I continued in that direction and found these words being thrust out of my throat, once again, without thinking. "Hey, what are you doing?"

Fortunately for me, the words woke me up a bit to the senselessness of that scenario; and just as fortunately, the two culprits could not hear me because they were so busy making a racket with their activity of piling up lumber into a tighter stack. I gave myself a moment or two to formulate just the right words to say to them.

What came out was "Hey, what are you doing?"

I could have smacked myself. These were the exact same words that could get me shot! This time, the two that were moving the lumber did hear me.

"Excuse me?" was the reply from the older man wearing jeans with a plaid shirt and a baseball cap.

"Oh, hello," I said, "I was wondering what you were doing. I guess I am a nosy neighbor."

Much to my relief, he chuckled and said, "We are piling up the lumber and covering it up before it rains."

"Ahh, well, good night." That's right, I remembered that it was going to rain for a couple of days in a row.

"Thanks for checking" were his words aimed at my retreating figure.

I waved and shuffled back to my house and once again felt a bit foolish. But I knew that the house was listening, and it knew that my intentions were good.

The blue house was being stripped from within, getting new walls, floors, and ceilings. We were having a few renovations done ourselves. It came time to dispose of some of the building materials left behind, as well as all the junk we were inspired to be rid of in the spirit of spring cleaning. We could haul all of this to the county transfer station, or we could take advantage of the generosity of the blue house. After all, just there in the driveway, beside the johnny house, was a huge dumpster that stood at least ten feet tall and twenty-five feet long. Even on tiptoes, no one could look in and see our few additions. My husband and I struggled with the dishonesty of using the dumpster. We went back and forth about this several times. After all, my whole life I usually got caught when trying to do something dishonest. On the other hand, I was the one that "saved" the house, and this would be a very nice way of rewarding me.

We finally got up the courage to dispose of our rubbish at the blue house's dumpster. Our courage was bolstered by the fact that it was under the cover of darkness. I suggested that we use the wheelbarrow to save a few trips. My husband said, "No, that would be too obvious." That got us to giggling. We then had to plan what to do if a car drove by as we were transporting lumber and broken furniture. We decided to simply drop it where we were and just act like we were taking a walk. I made sure that I took my apron off before we got started. Each of us made three trips without incident. One time, I thought I heard a car coming and jumped into the shadow of the johnny house. On another trip, we both had to carry a large piece of plywood together. I got spooked again and started hissing at my husband that we needed to drop it. Poor guy was walking backward, and I got so agitated that I started steering him toward the grass by tilting the plywood. He stumbled about, holding his own. By this time, we were both huffing and puffing, perspiring, and jumping at every noise that sounded like car tires on asphalt.

Not only was it nerve-racking to be prepared to "drop it, duck, and hide," we also cringed every time the debris was tipped into the dumpster and hit bottom with a loud *kaclunk*. We paused a few seconds after each *kaclunk*, looked quickly from house to house to see if anyone had turned on their front porch light or to see if anyone had ventured out to investigate the noise. We would scrap the operation if there were any signs of trouble.

One last trip to our house to assess the progress made us suddenly bold. We had enough of this being cautious to a fault. What the heck, let's pile it on the wheelbarrow. We both began piling the remaining debris as high as the wheelbarrow would allow, all on and not a scrap left. The last trip was quite a contrast to the previous ones. My husband and I started laughing and talking out loud. Suddenly we did not care if the neighbors saw what we were up to. Then a car actually did start to come our direction. Panic struck us both at the same time, and we started jogging with this precarious load on the barrow. I would shove and adjust with each jog of the barrow and shift of load. My husband just kept pushing faster and faster. We made it to the shadow of the johnny house once again and took cover. I had to cover my mouth to push back the giggles. My husband leaned over his knees to catch his breath, false alarm. The car turned into a driveway before reaching the sight of us.

The blue house had been magnanimous, however, as it watched over us, probably with amusement. With our last trip to the dumpster, I saluted the house and said, "Blue house, I think we're even now."

Church Lady

$\mathbb{W}$ith scribbled list in hand, I started in the direction of the tall kitchen trash bags when an announcement came over the intercom.

"Attention, Walmart shoppers. Would you like a free paring knife? We are giving away free paring knives today at Walmart. Please head over to the men's department to the covered podium to claim your knife. We will be giving them to everyone over the age of eighteen. You have four minutes to make your way to the covered podium in the men's department."

Hmmm, I thought, *I could use another paring knife.* I had never heard of Walmart giving away any merchandise. I wondered what that's about. Was it worth turning around to cross to other side of this mammoth store?

Another announcement came on telling us that time was running out, and we must get ourselves over to the men's department in the next two minutes. Well, of course, with an announcement like that, a sudden urge to hurry over struck quite a few shoppers, including me. We streamed over, some with empty carts, some with full, some with children, some with spouses in tow. I thought to throw some odd item in my cart so that no one would take off with it after I parked it against a rack of sweatpants.

Shortly thereafter, an announcement had us anticipating the announcer coming to the cloth-covered podium in a matter of seconds. From the atmosphere created by these few announcements, most of us felt we had won a contest by making it to the podium before the announcer had.

And there she was, a jolly, roly-poly lady with a freshly stiffened hairdo and fiercely penciled eyebrows. Her enthusiasm for her job and the excitement she projected made us all in a happy mood. I expected to simply reach with outstretched hand to claim my paring knife. I was prepared to present my driver's license to prove that I was over eighteen. My youngest son is almost eighteen, but you never know how serious this little lady was when it came to handing out free paring knives.

Now that she had us all gathered around her, she proceeded to ask for just five minutes of our time to demonstrate this wonderfully sharp knife that could cut through a metal can, a piece of wood, and still cut translucent slices of tomato after all that punishment. She whipped the cloth off the podium and exposed her workstation. We all watched her slice tomatoes, then hack into a piece of wood, saw into the metal head of an iron hammer, squeeze juice out of an orange with a little gadget, and listened and laughed at her jokes. The one I remember was how the knife had a lifetime guarantee, and if it ever got dull, we just had to send it right back to the company, and they would send a replacement. The joke part was "Now wouldn't that be great if we had that kind of guarantee with our husbands—when they get dull, just send 'em back and we get a replacement!" Not nice but funny.

This saleslady had our attention, and I could see many people digging out their wallets to buy this unbelievable knife made believable before our eyes. Not only that, it was getting better by the second because she was willing to throw in an extra knife, plus another paring knife, plus a filleting knife (which I didn't need), and of course, since we were probably going to give away our extra knife, she would replace it for us with a third knife. We would get these two wonderful plastic orange juicer gadgets that we all knew how to use now that she showed us. Our hearts were racing and fingers getting sweaty with all this free stuff coming our way. The real cause of the sweat was that it only applied to the first seven people that could get their money into her hand right then.

Thinking out loud, I said, "Gosh, I don't need that many knives. What am I going to do with all those knives?" I felt a sudden stab at my elbow. Beside me was a grandma that was rustling a scribbled note on an old receipt. It said, "I will go half with you." I looked in her eyes to see if she was serious. Her head was bobbing up and down. She was pointing to her wallet. I made an instant decision. "Okay," I mouthed. "I'll meet you at the flannel shirts over there," using my head to direct her attention.

I was thrown off guard for a moment when I heard her cell phone ring. She answered it and then started walking off down the aisle. First of all, she didn't look like a cell-phone-toting kind of grandma, and secondly, would she return to keep her end of the deal? Money was being flung toward our saleslady, and I got caught up again in the excitement. Logic was overcome with a "free stuff" mentality. I forked over my $19.99 to receive a bag of boxed knives. I am not sure if I was number six or seven in this rush to get the extra goodies, and I don't know that our saleslady was counting anyway. She probably learned at knife-selling school that a little competition made a sale more exciting, creating a frenzy of activity.

It must have been a short call, or else my grandma buddy cut it short. Soon she was at my elbow again, and we went between the flannel shirts to make good on our deal. The only problem was, there was an odd number of knives. I felt bad about shorting her, so I threw in the free orange juicer and the extra paring knife besides the fillet knife and the original amazing knife. I kept the free-paring knife and two amazing knives.

"What if the saleslady sees us?" I asked with some concern.

"Oh, honey, this is America!" Grandma squealed aloud but not too loudly to call attention to our dealings.

Despite my doubts about the equity of the deal, my grandma buddy was excited and grateful. She asked me, "What church do you go to?" I was at a loss for words because it was so out of context with what our business dealings were at the moment. I looked up from my plastic bag of knives and was silent for a long second. I weighed my options. There were none. What else could I do but tell her? So I shared that information.

She gleefully said, "I knew that you were a church lady!"

"How's that?" I asked.

"Well, you're wearing a skirt."

Sure enough, looking down, I saw that I was wearing my blue-jean skirt, a blouse, and a lightweight sweater. She was wearing a similar outfit. I had no idea what church ladies wore to Walmart. I wasn't even sure what a church lady was. I did find out that she was a church lady and introduced herself as Sister Grace.

She gave me a hug right there and said, "I know this is a blessed day. I feel blessed to have these knives and only pay half for them. The Lord is good."

I had to agree with her on that and smiled to myself to know that I looked like a church lady that day.

Car Wrecks and Tickets

I haven't had too many wrecks as a driver. Generally, I drive like a granny, following the speed limit, perhaps adding five miles to what is posted. I stop at the red light before turning right. I don't switch lanes in the middle of an intersection. However, if someone is following me too closely, I will tap my brakes a few times to warn them off.

I didn't get my driver's license until the summer after my sixteenth birthday in April. This was due to me not starting driver's education at North Mecklenburg High School until my actual sixteenth birthday. I remember the first time I sat behind the wheel. I never had driven before, so this was quite a test of my nerves and the teacher's nerves. My mom would complain about people slowing down excessively to make a left-hand turn. I remembered that complaint when the instructor told me to turn left, which I did, but based on what my mom complained about, I didn't use my brakes. I figured I didn't have to slow down to turn left, so I didn't. The instructor barked at me that I needed to use the brakes when I turned left. I was puzzled by that, but I did have the sensation that I might not successfully make that left turn. Fortunately, the instructor applied his set of brakes for me so we wouldn't end up in the ditch. He did inform me that I need to use the brakes, by the way.

My mom urged my dad to take me out to practice my driving. Off we go down Mayes Road. I kept steady, staying in the lane. There was a turtle in the road. I ran over it. My dad suddenly raised his knee and hit his head with his hand as he exclaimed, "Jesus Christ, you just ran over a turtle!" I didn't realize that I could swerve a bit to avoid the turtle.

My first wreck was the first week of school. The bus route was so long, and seeing that I was the first one on the bus and the last one off, my mom convinced my dad that I should be able to drive to school to avoid the two hours on the bus. The bus route took us down miles of country roads to pick up one or two students that stood at the end of a gravel drive. Then we had to backtrack to do the same for a few more students down another remote road, repeating this until we had maybe a half bus full before heading to school.

The first day I drove to school, I was backing out of the parking space but turned too soon so that my front bumper gouged out the passenger side of the neighboring car. I had so little experience driving that I didn't dare move the car. Instead, I went to the office to get some help. The assistant principal came out to help, only to be faced with a hysterical girl that was wailing about how her mother was going to kill her. I stayed calm, gave her my dad's name and number, and went home with one wreck under my belt. The mom did call my dad and screamed at him. He simply said, "Well, that's why I have insurance." I never made that same mistake again! It surprised me that my dad didn't yell at me.

The next wreck came thirty years later. I was behind a car that was supposed to yield to oncoming traffic while turning right. My eyes were focused on the oncoming traffic coming from the left. Not seeing any cars coming, I went ahead and turned right, not realizing that the driver in front of me did not have the same reflexes that I had when it came to entering a road. He had not even begun to turn right, so I hit him from behind. Instead of holding up the cars behind us, I suggested we go to the next neighborhood to exchange information. Before I even got home, he had called my home to verify the number and told the whole wreck story to my husband. Apparently, the man had called home to let his family know what happened. They told him he was a fool to trust that I had given him the correct information, and he better call the number I gave him to see if it was authentic. I had no idea that people would give out false information and leave the other person holding the bag, so to speak.

As a young mother, I took aerobics classes at the YMCA. My new baby came along with me, staying in the nursery during the class. This particular morning, I was running late, so I used bad judgment and went through a yellow light that turned red. I didn't even see the policeman behind me. He pulled me over, saw the baby, and gave me a lecture right then and there. I was humiliated, went on to the YMCA, but fell into weeping as I pulled into the parking lot. I just turned around and went home. I have avoided going through yellow lights ever since. If I can't avoid going through one, I do take look in the rearview mirror to check for any patrol cars behind me.

More recently, I went to Lowe's for a quick shopping trip. I was out within fifteen minutes. I looked for my car and found a blue Subaru in the spot I left it, but my brain said, "This is not my car!" Someone had sideswiped me and left a long dent and scrape on my front side panel. I was furious, especially since the parking place adjacent to me was reserved for vets. When the policeman came, he looked at the damage and announced that it was at the height of a truck bumper, and there was a bit of white paint on the upper side of the dent. Within the time the driver of the truck managed to back his truck into the parking spot and simultaneously damaged my car and the time I emerged from my shopping at Lowe's, the culprit had driven off—no note, no apologies, nothing!

After the policeman got my information and filled in the police report, I took it upon myself to march up and down the parking lot, looking for a truck with a damaged bumper. After all, the truck driver was at Lowe's to shop also, right? Maybe he just moseyed on down to another parking spot as if nothing happened. I had no luck finding a white truck with a damaged bumper. I gave up, went home, and called my insurance company. After all, that's why I have insurance.

Winter in Holland

I f you have seen postcards of Holland depicting long-ago ice-skaters on the canals, you will see layers of black wool pants, coats, skirts, hats, all for practical warmth, but streaming in the wind is a beautifully colorful warm scarf wrapped several times around the skater's neck.

That was long ago, but nowadays, the outerwear is not much different except in style. Black shoes, pants, coats, hats, and shoes seem to be the uniform, and the scarf adds distinction between people. It is cold in Holland in the winter. The skies hang low with grey clouds. The wind blows fiercely across the land. The rain pelts down in spurts. Everyone is prepared for any kind of weather. They carry on with their lives despite the weather since that is the life there. The Dutch hop on their bikes to cycle to the grocery store or to school and work. They pump their legs harder when cycling into head winds but get a swift return trip with the wind at their backs.

As soon as the sun comes out, people venture outside. They sit on the park benches, walk through the streets, woods, or dunes, catching any ray of sun that might find them. I saw a woman on the bus close her eyes and hold a smile that expressed her delight in finding a seat that allowed the sun to shine on her face. These sunny minutes or even fleeting moments are precious.

Even though the winter weather is grey, the fields are bright green, the village buildings have window and door frames painted bright but not gaudy colors. There are plants in the large picture windows, flowering pots in small gardens, even a few garden ornaments that express humor and color. I think this is the way the Dutch cope. They have splashes of color throughout their lives.

Between Christmas and New Year's Eve, I visited my sister, Fransje, who lives in Holland. She lives in a small town near the coast south of Rotterdam. We visited other nearby small towns in rural Holland. Fransje and I walked the cobbled sidewalks and brick streets, slowly taking in the feel of the town. What stood out to me was that most houses and businesses have the largest windows possible, allowing in as much light as possible. The Christmas decorations on the deep window sills were most tastefully displayed with items old and new, creatively made from natural materials such as wood, greenery, shells, and even bark from trees. I saw very little glitter or glowing bulbs. It was so simple that it could be left out for weeks past Christmas, and it would still be a beautiful winter display.

A lonely stone and wood windmill from long ago stood at the edge of town. In the distance stood the windmill fields of today, standing tall and looking like giant white seagull sculptures, metal, cold, and silent. What a contrast. I had a sudden affection for the remaining reminder of the all-important village windmill used to grind wheat into flour so long ago.

One day, we went to a nearby town with the sole mission of visiting the food truck, that offered raw fish as well as fresh fried fish. The smells coming from the fryer made our wait even more impatient. We ordered a large portion of fried cod to share, nothing else. We sat on a nearby bench, enjoying the fish nearly as much as the sun. It was hard to get up and get going since the simple experience was so delightful even though pedestrians walked by in front and behind our bench. We sat for a few minutes more, enjoying the view of the town canal with its small boats tied up, each uniquely and colorfully painted. We reluctantly gathered our greasy napkins, wiped the telltale signs from our lips, and disposed of our trash. Within seconds, someone else slid onto the bench even as we were just steps away. It was their turn to enjoy the simple basking in the sun and tasty morsels of hot fried cod.

My Mountain Days

Franklin Time

⌘

What is Franklin Time? I have come to discover the meaning of Franklin Time in the past twelve months I have come to live here. The meaning of that term has evolved in my mind from a very basic level to a more complex level. Let me tell you about Franklin Time.

I moved here after forty-five years of living in Atlanta, Georgia, having had enough of being in a large city. I had visited Franklin over the last twenty-two years since my mom moved here to be in the mountains. These North Carolina mountains reminded her of her early years living in Indonesia, holding those times dear to her heart. Indonesia was a Dutch colony, with its mountains and tropical climate, a sharp contrast to her native Holland, which offered a flat, cold, grey environment.

When my mom first moved to Franklin, I remember her feeling a bit frustrated because she had hired someone to do some carpentry work in her 1920s house. Although the man was as nice as could be, his timing on completing the job was not her idea of timing. I suggested I put a fire under him, but she said, "No, dear, everyone here is on Franklin Time." I interpreted that to be that they would make the time to do things as it suited them. I must admit that the

141

wait was worth it because the outcome was proof of care and pride on the part of the carpenter.

When I moved here, I found myself facing the same Franklin Time dilemma that she had. Franklin Time has, in the meantime, taken on a different guise for me. I found that it is not my initial basic definition of doing things when it suits people. Franklin Time means that I can go to the post office, and the postal workers are friendly and speak more than two words to me, not showing any sign of hurrying me along to get to the next customer. Besides that, when the line gets more than few, someone appears and opens another window. Each time I go to the post office, I embrace Franklin Time and feel no irritation with the elderly customers that spend an extra few minutes chatting with the postal worker about their well-being or grandchildren or the weather. I just stand there, embracing Franklin Time.

When it took months for my new exterior doors to get measured, remeasured, and ordered, I got over my feeling of impatience because the contact at the local big box store would call me every week to let me know the status of the door order. To know that I was not forgotten, put me back on track with Franklin Time. It would get done when it would get done. Once again, the wait was worth it because the installation crew came out and, in one day, installed my two new doors, a window, and replaced siding on two exterior walls. Done!

Franklin Time means when you ask questions at the store, you are treated with patience and kindness and spoken to as if you are a friend. It means that my mom can go to the same cashier at Ingles, and the cashier knows where to find her quarters and nickels on one side of her wallet and her pennies and dimes in the other. It means that the butcher will help her by grinding suet for her birds, kindly sharing a few personal words as part of the service.

Franklin Time means that as you walk along the Greenway, most everyone greets you with a smile, a nod, a direct look into your face. It means that the gathering at the end of the day at the dog park for dog owners is a time of relaxation, comparing dog companions, admiring the qualities the dogs express, and a big dose of laughter and camaraderie as a reward for carving out some Franklin Time.

Franklin Time means that the volunteers at the Greenway will take time off task to show you where the beaver lodge is and explain why the dam is broken down each day. It means you can find kindness rocks hidden in the tall grass along the river and elsewhere because someone took time and thought into creating a painted rock that would become a little surprise package of kindness, anticipating the excitement over its discovery. Franklin Time means that I can feel perfectly comfortable going to the summer concerts by myself and still feel included because the air is filled with infectious enjoyment. Watching young children dance to the oldies but goodies shows that music speaks to everyone.

It means that when my sewer backed up and the rooter company showed up to save the day, they knew the window washer who came shortly thereafter because they both have sons on the same baseball team which they coach together. I could see through my window that the men stood in a circle, stopping to carve out some Franklin Time, which has the same value as work time. The doctor's office bookkeeper stopped midwork to patiently explain the Medicare billing system that was confusing as all heck to me. She kindly agreed that it was confusing, making me feel less stupid than when I came in just moments prior. Most importantly, it means that when your security lights come on late at night, it is not a prowler that can throw fear into your heart; but the ring-tailed, black-masked prowler that is more interested in the bird feeder than whatever you might hold precious in your house. I now turn off the interior lights, taking time to watch with delight, my night visitors that go through all kinds of antics to get to their midnight snack.

Franklin Time means things get done but are wrapped up with respect, kindness, consideration, and the gift of precious time set aside for one another. So if you are not experiencing Franklin Time, you will when you recognize it for what it simply is.

Baling Hay

❧

What is that noise? I wondered to myself. My windows were wide open, welcoming the summer breezes that made my curtains billow up and down and sideways, all at the same time. I went to the window and peered out. Nothing in sight. It sounded like a mower, the big tractor kind. It sounded so close by. Is the farmer finally cutting the tall grass on the vacant lots of this former pasture that I now call home?

I was told a few weeks earlier that the vacant lots, over twenty-five of them, mostly adjoining one another, were going to be mowed and baled in the near future. I had mixed feelings about the sea of tall grass being slashed. I enjoyed seeing the grass respond to the weather.

My neighbor, who uses his riding mower to cut my yard, warned me that he ran over several snakes and rats while mowing the roadside. I am not afraid of rats and snakes. The snakes keep the rat population down, and generally rats run for it when they sense a larger body invading their territory. I knew to be cautious when cutting the wild daisies that stood tall among the grass, brambles, and purple-flowered weeds. I did wonder as I stood, patiently snipping the slender stems of the daisies, are there more weeds than grass in this field long neglected? Do cows have tongues made of leather that can munch through the less desirable vegetation? Are the daisies like dessert to them? I know so little about country life, having spent the last forty-five years in the big city of Atlanta.

There it is! The farmer on his mower, coming over the rise of the land. Sound travels over hill and dale whereas vision doesn't. I wondered how long it would take to cut all these acres. By the end of the day, everything was cut, stems and stalks lying in parallel rows. The next day, after the sun had dried the fields, the farmer appeared with another apparatus. I stood at the window again, seeing him move slowly down one row after another with a spinning attachment that sent the parallel piles into heaps clustered closer together.

The third day, there were numerous trucks, a forklift, and a baler that had a drum-shaped attachment at the back. By the time I had gotten dressed and started down the quarter mile gravel road, I saw six huge rolls of hay on the side of the road. I lowered my car window as I approached the line of bales to snap a picture with my phone camera. The fellow with the forklift waited patiently while I fumbled with my phone. My efficiency declined with every moment of him waiting. I moved on down the road after giving the forklift fellow a wave, trying to indicate my appreciation for his patience.

By the time I got back from town, most of the fields were baled. The bales were moved to a nearby barn that was known to be home to rats galore. So I suppose, the rats and snakes relocate by seeking refuge in the rat barn as long as they are quick enough at the first rumble of the tractor motor to avoid blades, spinning wheels, or being swept up into the baling device. In a few months, the rats, snakes, and I will once again hear the rumble of the mower and move into position, ready to watch or to flee.

Pumpkins, Cows, and Children

As a volunteer, I like to get to school at least fifteen minutes early before picking up my second grade reading groups. I teach three groups for thirty minutes each. This morning, I stood at the top of the stairwell two stories up. This is where I conduct my teaching of reading skills, in a bump-out of the stairwell where a table and seven chairs are ready to receive my students.

Standing at the second story railing, I looked out the large window overlooking a cow pasture. What a delight to look out and see the cows in the pasture, concentrating on nibbling whatever green stems and shoots are at their hooves. They shuffle along peacefully, oblivious to the several hundred youngsters who are housed in the elementary school adjacent to the pasture. On occasion, if I can observe the cows for more than a few seconds, they raise their heads to take note of where the rest of their herd mates are. I notice that they all are standing in the same direction. I notice that at times, once they have their fill of pasture grass, they will rest on the ground, all of them, with their jaws chewing their cud, a constant motion in a crisscross fashion rather than the usual up and down meeting of the jaws.

These are the perks of living in a rural mountain community. The residents who have lived here all their lives may not give the cows a second look. It is a wonderful country thing to look all around and be in a peaceful atmosphere rather than the frenetic setting of a large city. I know since I've been there, done that.

Last week, my lesson was based on the life cycle of the pumpkin. I thought that appropriate since Halloween was upon us. I posed a question to the students after reading that pumpkins grow on a vine. The vine is pretty thick, as thick as the cut stem. I asked, "How would I get the pumpkin off the vine?"

Most of the children knew, without a second thought, that you would need a saw or a sharp knife. One student gave me a very knowledgeable and certain answer because his dad cuts pumpkins off the vine from their garden.

The student said, "My dad uses a lopper, you know, what you use to cut branches with."

I nodded to let him know I knew what he was talking about. He continued, "Yeah, it's good for cutting chicken heads off too."

My reaction must have been priceless because all six children took one look at the expression on my face and burst out in laughter.

He said, "No, no, I meant the rooster!"

I said, "Whether a rooster or a chicken, believe me, I don't want to hear about it! I won't be able to get the image out of my brain!"

I did let out a chuckle, so the kids knew that they weren't in trouble. Obviously, they knew the chicken-and-lopper method firsthand whereas this was the first time I had ever heard of such a thing. I suppose a lopper is more efficient than an axe and a tree stump. The humor in that situation made us all laugh and brought us together in a special way.

Many of these children grow up learning practical solutions to living the country life. They know about good fishing spots, think nothing of a deer being brought home to be processed, fetch eggs from the chicken coop, and cope with their dogs coming home reeking of skunk. I know this because over the last two years, they have shared their stories, and I listen. I love to hear them express themselves, developing communication skills through telling their stories.

And I continue to listen. Some have told me without a shred of embarrassment how they got little sleep the night before because they had to sleep at Meemaw's house instead of their own because their mama or daddy, or both, didn't come home last night. They wondered aloud where they would sleep tonight.

I notice that a few students wear the same shirt for several days, stained with the food from today and the days before. One child has such dirty fingernails, but I listen to him read. I never saw his fingernails clean. I have one student who missed two or three days of school a week because he is homeless. That's what I have been told, but not from him. He proudly called attention to his new suede boots that had leather lacings. I admired them and told him that they looked good and warm and so new. And I listen to him read, struggling with words, but I praise him for not giving up and figuring out the sounds that make the words.

I was told that one of my students lives with grandma in a camper in an RV park. I asked his reading group to tell of the most unusual place that they have eaten dinner after reading a story about crazy places to eat, giving them an example of maybe sitting on a rock outside. That student said he did that every day. All I could say was how lucky he was to enjoy his dinner outside.

I had to report to the counselor how one student was left alone the night before. I found this out as I observed him nodding off during my group time. I asked him if he went to bed late last night. He said, "Yes, because my mom and dad were gone to work and left me alone with the dog, but I was afraid of the rat that is in the house. It could bite me." To be fair, I didn't know how long the child was left alone or if the rat was actually a rat or maybe a mouse in the house. Any amount of time a child is left alone might seem like an eternity, never mind having only a dog for protection from the rat.

By my estimation, about one fourth of the students get food parcels on Thursdays. These are in paper bags, clearly marked, sitting in a pile outside the classroom doors. Carenet, a local charity, provides this food so that the children will have food over the weekend. I have been told that the bus drivers observe some of the students hiding their food in the woods before going into their homes. These are the skills that these children have developed to cope.

These are unique situations for a small number of students. I cannot paint a picture showing that all the students have it rough at home. Most come from very loving families. I have seen firsthand how the community comes together to provide the essentials for local families in need. There are area churches that conduct food and clothing drives. There are businesses that step up to raise funds that are, in turn, given to local charities that know where the funds are most needed. There are individuals that donate schools supplies to the Macon County schools. They will not depend on government agencies to meet the needs of the local community. Instead of waiting, they take action.

I am part of the community that is meeting the need at the nearby elementary school. I do what I do best, teach reading and listen to the children. The teachers express their gratitude regularly, and in turn, I express my gratitude for giving me a purpose. Amen.

Christmas Busyness

❧

The local paper announced community Christmas activities. Some were church sponsored, some community sponsored, and some were as simple as neighborly people having an event to share with anyone who might want to explore new holiday-related activities.

My Saturday began with a visit to the Cowee School Christmas event. I went last year and enjoyed it, so I made the short jaunt from my home. The volunteers directed me to the nearest parking spot. I climbed the steps into the former elementary school to be greeted by a friendly lady explaining to me what there was to see. The hubbub was at a pretty high level. The activities appealed to all ages from the sale of knitted caps, handmade scented soaps, crafted pottery, jewelry, and wooden kitchen tools, to hands-on woodworking fun for the kids. They could make a toy at Grandpa's Workshop, and work away they did, busy with saws and hammers.

I made my way slowly and carefully past bunches of people through the toy museum room, the quilt guild room, and the two art studios that had friendly hosts ready to answer questions. I enjoyed a few moments of banjo music that was remarkably good from the preteen youngster that offered Christmas tunes and carols. I got to the end of the hallway and found a table of painted rocks. This would be a fun thing to take back to the grandkids. I plucked up and examined several and weighed my options of which painted rocks would match the personality of my three grandkids whom I would see soon. Honestly, my choices were gut choices, matching the feeling they projected with the child that would receive it. This string of lights painted on the rock with "Be Merry and Bright" looked like Kayla, this Santa one suited Collin, and this yellow flowery one would go well with Kinsley who liked to sing "You Are My Sunshine" anytime she has an audience.

My visit ended in the old school cafeteria where there was a variety of soup, bread, and dessert choices for a cheap lunch. I sat beside a man who looked alone; and sure enough, our conversation finally landed on how his wife died last year and how difficult it was to run his wood furniture business, care for the pets and run the household. He came to Cowee School to help with Grandpa's Workshop at the request of another artistic volunteer. We parted ways with him giving me his business card and us wishing each other a good rest of the day. It was a friendly and simple encounter. Funny though, he said I had an accent. What? Okay, I'm not from the North Carolina mountains, but I never thought I had an accent—well, maybe an accent that is just not from around here.

My next stop was to a pottery show out in the countryside. It was advertised on the Franklin What's Happening Facebook page and not terribly far from where I lived. The roads were very curvy, and few other cars were using it. I began to wonder if it was a hoax but finally saw a small arrow pointing toward the sale, and after a few more miles, another sign to let me know I was going the right direction. When I turned off the road, I ended up on a gravel road through the woods and drove through a wide, shallow creek, then finally to a wooded clearing with some rustic buildings scattered about. There were maybe thirty people milling around, some sitting at a picnic table eating baked potatoes and sipping hot drinks.

There were a few kids running around wildly, having a delightful time being loud and bossy. They easily managed to trip trop over the narrow bridge that crossed them to the other side of the creek. They were chasing each other through a grassy area, high stepping it through the tall grass, then dodging the slender saplings and briars that grabbed hold of their pants. They seemed to run aimlessly, then chase each other around the several thick tree trunks of the mature trees left standing in the clearing. How refreshing to see children let loose, their lungs and legs at full tilt.

I visited three areas where mostly pottery was sold, plus some homemade scented soap. The outbuildings were quaint, weathered board structures with walls of sturdy shelves to display pottery pieces. I viewed them with interest and meandered to the next shelter. I chatted with the sellers and enjoyed the thick moss under my feet. The low cloudy sky made it feel intimate, along with the woods surrounding the clearing. It was a contrast to the Cowee School which was full of the droning noise of people, shuffling feet, and background music. This place had a very slow pace, people enjoying each other's company. The conversations were muffled, relaxed. The woodsy smell was accentuated with the moist decay of fallen leaves and an additional layer of smoke from the smoldering firepit.

I saw one of the teachers I work with and her husband. We stood very comfortably on that mossy carpet, which really impressed me by how thick it was. I kept thinking about the moss with its bright green color and bouncy feel, of all things, even while exchanging pleasantries. I strolled leisurely back to my car where there was a woman cleaning her work boots out of the back of her truck which was parked beside my car. So I chatted with her. I made a comment that I could see a fancy sports car parked just on the other side of the creek. She said the driver probably didn't know how deep the flow of water was, but it was never deeper than a few inches. She shared that her boots are very old because she has a hard time finding her shoe size, which she admitted was large and wide. I climbed into my car, drove through the shallow water, and found my way home with my bag containing a small bar of handmade oatmeal soap. I hummed Christmas tunes the rest of the afternoon.

Anonymous

— ✺ —

I prefer fast-food restaurants giving me a number for my order rather than asking for my name. I like to remain anonymous. Besides, they never do understand my name and want to call me Martina. I am not Martina!

That doesn't keep me away from one particular name-asking restaurant. The only thing I order from their menu is a large order of fries. On my way to Atlanta from Franklin, I stopped by a chicken fast-food restaurant in Clayton, Georgia. It was 10:23 a.m. I know that because after using the restroom, I went to the counter to order my fries. I asked if they had fries for sale yet. The cashier said no, it was 10:23 a.m., and they wouldn't be serving fries until 10:30 a.m. I asked if I could go ahead and place an order. Another cashier decided to get in on the conversation and said that no, I would have to wait until 10:30 a.m., and then it would be another ten minutes before the fries were ready.

My next question was where I would find the same restaurant between Clayton and Atlanta. It was Cornelia, but I have never exited at Cornelia, and with these small towns, you never know if the fast-food places are near the exit or all the way in town. I took a chance and exited, only to be left high and dry on which way to turn. I chose right, thinking that was the way to the town of Cornelia, if the store was not near the exit ramp. No sign of the restaurant, so after a couple of miles, I spotted a good turnaround at a thrift store. A lady was exiting her car in the parking lot, so I cruised up to her and rolled down my window and asked her the location of the chicken restaurant. She looked confused. I'm not sure if she was confused because she didn't know there was one in Cornelia or that she did know but couldn't picture in her mind where it was. She kindly offered to go into the store and ask, then come out to tell me.

I realized seconds later that I should be the one to go in and inquire. Good thing I did because when I went in, the two folks behind the counter looked perplexed, perhaps not understanding the question or wondering why this lady took it upon herself to come in to ask the question and then deliver the answer. I piped up that I was the one who asked where the restaurant was. I must have been more clear with the question than the kind lady because all perplexity was erased from their faces, and they simply said that it was in front of the Walmart, back toward the highway. I know I passed the Walmart but never saw it. A mystery, but after a few niceties, I went on my way to find that, yes, it was in the same parking lot as Walmart but camouflaged by a row of leafy trees.

After checking out the restroom, once again, I got in line to order my large waffle fries. The gal behind the counter asked for my name. She looked baffled when I said I don't give out my name. "Well, please make up a name so that when your order comes up, they can call out a name." I drew a complete blank on a fake name to give, so for once, I was mute and just raised my hands up in that questioning way people do to let people know that they don't know. I was so concerned that I would promptly forget my fake name, that I would never get my waffle fries, or if I finally shook myself awake after hearing my fake name numerous times, the fries would be cold. She looked perturbed, not any way a cashier is supposed to act because they are all about customer service and cheerfulness. She was not cheerful and swiveled on her heels to tell the waffle fry person that Ms. No Name wanted a large waffle fry.

While I was waiting for my order, I thought, *Gosh, I suppose I could have named myself Large Fries.* It wasn't like I had five items to pick up, just the one. My plan was suddenly hatched for the next encounter of extracting my name. I'll just say, "Call me Large Fries,'" and then either laugh or look dead serious.

After that stream of thoughts, I heard someone announce, "Large Fries." I said, "That's me!" See? It worked.

Mourning the Mountains

⟶ ✎ ⟵

I mourn the mountains before I leave so soon. I realize now that has been my troubled feelings these last few weeks. I am more attached to the land I live on, walk on, drive through than perhaps even I know.

I feel tears well up in my eyes, and my throat feels restricted as I snuffle back the need to cry, a real cry. I am not allowing myself to cry a real cry. Instead, I write at my computer, feeling a trickle of warm salt tears roll down my cheek. Then it is the other eye's turn to allow its splash to be pulled over the edge of my lid and follow the curve of my cheek to rest at my jaw. The itch is too much for me, so a trip to the tissue box is all I need to reset my moody mood. I have tricked myself out of my misery once again.

Now that I have decided to move back to the city, I am viewing what I am leaving behind with new eyes, fresh perspective. I look out my front window, obscured with white cotton sheers that let in light and softened outlines of green grass, hard brown limbs, and patches of red clay where grass seed has been rejected by the land.

I look out the back of the house and view the squat but impressive Appalachian Mountains giving me a sense of permanence and strength, of settling and protection. The sun sets on these ranges with me feeling confident that they will be there in the morning, receiving the first morning rays that change the outline, color, and shadowing, fooling the human eye into seeing something different from minute to minute. They may be gently surrounded by fog in the morning or brightly lit by the sun. The seasonal colors can be intense or sparse, but the mountains remain the same foundation.

When I go to the town's landfill, I see beyond the dumpsters of trash, recyclables, or mounds of yard waste to the horizon that is fringed with mountains, smooth-topped old mountains of the east. When I go to the library, I see different mountains from the parking lot or a more isolated view from the riverwalk located in the valley below the library. The valley holds the river that meanders through soft clay, around granite rocks, tree roots exposed, and spewing up on its banks natural debris after heavy rainfall, covering up the park benches with mounds of twigs, pine straw, vines, and silt. The walk offers a trail that follows the river but then darts off to the right to follow the sharp incline back to the library.

I turn onto my gravel road and am greeted with a view of my pastureland neighborhood amid protective mountains. I see our five modest houses huddled close to the ground, each surrounded by empty lots that was the vision of the developer to be a neighborhood of some thirty homes. Years later, the few of us that call this land home are smugly happy that no one else is interested in the land on which to build. It is a mystery to me, coming from the city, but obvious to the local folks. Why pay for land that does not look down upon the valley but instead, *is* the valley? Why pay a city price for a country lot?

This home meets my need of isolation, peace, and few distractions, but at the same time, offers neighbors that look out for one another and run to help if called. This is the perfect balance for me. I found my peace at last which readied me to return to the city where my friends and family reside. I hope I am able to adjust to the drone and hubbub of city life. I can easily return for short spurts of time if I need the respite of these old mountains.

I have completed my mission, that of caring for my elderly mother in a way that allowed her to stay in her home as long as possible. She stubbornly stayed and stayed until it was time to face the fact that she could not care for herself properly for so many hours of the day and night. With great courage on both our parts, she settled into a care place. At the very least, she knew she was still surrounded by her beloved mountains, perhaps not in immediate view, but the knowledge that they were there seemed to be enough.

There were more reasons to come to the mountains than the single one pertaining to my mom's care. I needed the mountains and country life for myself. At the time, I didn't know that. Now I know. Now I see that I am a different person than the person I was. I attribute that to the fundamental kindness and caring shown to Mom and me, kindness and caring by the people in town at the grocery store, the bank, and the fast-food place. "Hon" is common in a greeting. A smile is not far behind. The sun sets and rises not only on the mountains, but on the people below, giving and sharing people. Those that need it eventually recognize the caring as a gift even more valuable than the gems found in the local mines. I will drive away with the mountains in my rearview mirror. I am leaving them, but they are not leaving me.

Being an Oma

Fall Ball

F all Ball has started. My four-year-old grandson has one
   season under his belt and has graduated to the field that
actually has stadium seating and a fence around the field. I
pull into the parking lot of the ball field and see that the lot is
full. I drive a bit further and find a spot off road on the crest
of the hill that overlooks the fields.

I see colorful uniforms of the various teams and spot the
orange and blue uniforms of Collin's team. I see some young
players being led quickly across the wet grass as parents have
made it just in time for the game to start. Warm-ups are over
for the stragglers.

Ten o'clock in the morning on the first fallish weather
day of the season makes me appreciate the cool temperatures.
The thin sun above makes the grass sparkle with the remaining dewdrops. I am delighted that my parking space is conveniently located close to a paved path down a steep bank. Last
year, I struggled with that bank and hoped and prayed that
I would not tumble head over heels on the slick pine straw
and camouflaged pine cones as I carried my chair to the fields
designated with only a backstop.

It is more a picnic ground with parents and siblings
lined up in chairs, along with coolers, strollers, and play-

things. Errant balls are not a threat to the spectators since the novice ballplayer struggles to see under the too large hat tilting downward. The bobbling, clumsy helmets make successful contact with the ball a challenge. Contact with the ball on the tee means a little tap that rolls the ball off to dribble in a random direction.

Oh, it is fun and funny to see the antics of the boys. Rather than knowing roles and strategies at this beginner stage, a whole pack of boys runs after the same dribbled ball and fight over who can grab it. The triumphant boy simply stands there, not knowing what to do next with the prize. Outfielders dig or write in the dirt. Some turn their backs to the action while an airplane distracts them. Their attention span is limited as is typical with that age group.

I make my way down the paved, less-sloped path, sans chair, this season. My sandaled feet are refreshingly dampened by the morning dew on the grass that skirts the fenced-in field. There is a slight chill in the air, and I am glad I am wearing a long-sleeved shirt. The balance between the weak warmth of the sun on my shoulders and the cool morning breeze is delightful.

Now the game begins. It is the beginning of the season, and the players have not lost their habits from last year. There is still a pack of players running after the ball. The outfielders might as well be out of the field all together. Some parents seem mortified that their son is twirling, hopping, fighting imaginary super villains and such things that small boys do when bored. The parents encourage the little ones by shouting to them to "run to first!" The coaches are endlessly patient and generous with "high fives."

The game is over, and no one knows the score. The boys are learning the essential rules of the game, and the score is not important at this point. What seems more important to the young player is the juice pouch and crackers at the end of the game. To see eleven little boys swinging their legs under the picnic table, munching on crackers, and squirting juice playfully out of the juice pouch is just as fun to watch as the antics on the field.

The coach awards the game ball to a player that has shown outstanding ball game participation. The youngster is so unprepared with this honor that he takes his juice pouch and the game ball and sidles up to Mom, pressing close to her legs, hoping to be less visible. Mom pats him on the shoulder while we clap and woohoo. He is thoroughly embarrassed. By season's end, the game ball holder will have learned the etiquette as the recipient, along with a few more ball strategies and skills. I smile.

Snow Day!

─────── ⌘ ───────

The children kept looking out the picture window overlooking the backyard and nearby woods. It was cold and cloudy. "Is it snowing yet?" they would take turns asking. I am standing in the background thinking to myself, *Is it supposed to snow today?* I had not a clue that it was supposed to snow. I seemed to be the last to know and oblivious to the weather forecast.

My job was to watch my three grandkids while their parents went to the mountains for a marriage retreat. I descended the mountain, and they in turn ascended to meet with their church pastor and numerous other couples at Brasstown Bald, about seventy miles to the north of Canton.

All was going quite smoothly on Saturday morning with each child coming down the steps in staggered time. Breakfast first, then see how they would compromise on what to watch on TV. The ages of three, eight, and twelve were quite a challenge to satisfy; but with minimal arguments, it was agreed to watch *Doc McStuffins*, then a hero cartoon and finally something more mature but still acceptable for youngest eyes and still please the twelve-year-old young lady.

The TV watching was short-lived because someone with eagle eyes spotted the first miniscule snowflake, which was actually more like a Styrofoam pellet. All four of us stood there, feeling a bit disappointed because it did not look promising for accumulation. After a few minutes, the high-pitched squealing began. All three emitted the same volume and pitch, making it indistinguishable which one was the loudest, but I feel confident it was the three-year-old who won that contest.

The snow pellets had turned to snowflakes, coming down in sudden volume. There was squealing and scrambling looking for snow boots, snow pants, gloves, coats, hats. The two older ones found their gear, and I saw them putting all this on right over their pajamas. I wouldn't be able to stop the momentum, so I let it go. Little Kinsley was frantic, not knowing what to do. But she did know where her snow boots were, and Kayla found her snow pants. Her coat was hanging on its usual hook at the back door, so the only dilemma was the lack of gloves or mittens.

What could I wear outside? I was ill prepared because of ignorance. The only thing I had going for me was that I could double up on socks and hope that my Mary Jane Skechers would give me enough traction and protection from the ever-increasing volume of snow. No hat, oh well. I did have gloves in my coat pocket.

By this time, the dogs knew something exciting was happening, and they added to the chaos by barking like mad. I said, "Let's take the dogs outside too!" Off we went, three children, one grandma, and two dogs on leashes that seemed to have super strength at pulling on the leash because the excitement that was infectious. We zigzagged through the side yard, with the dogs relieving themselves and prancing about until we thought it best to put them back in their crates while we walked through the park across the street, making the very first snowy footprints in the light layer of snow. Kinsley suddenly started wailing, saying, "My hands hurt, my hands hurt!" Well, yes, they would since she had no gloves. I gave her my gloves that looked like black-flapping birds, but they were better than nothing.

We strolled through the park and found that the slides there were super slippery with snow. Large patches of compressed snow were left on the three behineys after zipping down the snow-slick slide. Fortunately, I had my phone with me and could capture the mounting snow fall and activities with the camera. A shot of them sitting on a bench, three in a row, with heads tilted upward, trying to catch snowflakes on their tongues. Another of them with handfuls of snow that they scraped off the bench seats. I took a picture of Kinsley's hatless head that had snowflakes captured on the crown of her head and the curly tendrils around her face. Their faces grew red with exertion while exploring the possible ice patches near the road, the rapid pace of their meandering path, leaving Kinsley and me well behind. After forty-five minutes, someone had the bright idea to head home and have hot chocolate, just like they do in the movies, right? By then, my toes were cold; and without feeling and the idea of getting my flimsy shoes off and letting them heat up in the house was more enticing than hot chocolate.

The rest of the afternoon was spent in and out of doors. I found a pile of beach towels and spread them out at each doorway. Even though leaving boots outside was a good idea, it was not always remembered, plus their snow pants collected blobs of snow that fell off as they traipsed through the house to the essential bathroom.

Kayla and Collin found the saucer and the long plastic sled in the basement. Thank goodness they were a bright green and orange so that I could spot them from the same picture window that we stood at earlier, earnestly looking at the sky for signs of snow.

Kinsley happily found her gloves, but putting gloves on a three-year-old proved to be challenging. We came up with a method. She would spread her fingers apart as far as she possibly could while I stretched the glove wide to put over them. Nevertheless, numerous times, fingers and thumb shared the same finger pocket. If that happened, we would try again. Kinsley checked by pinching each fingertip and counting to five to make sure they were each in the right place. Those gloves were skimpy though. After spending a few minutes patting the snow, gathering handfuls, tossing it over the railing side, scraping it into mounds, eating handfuls of snow, with me reminding her to only eat the snow on the tabletop, experimenting in every imaginable way with the snow, she would pound on the door, needing to come in because her hands hurt. I promptly placed those soggy gloves on the floor vent in the bathroom. I continued to act as traffic cop, making sure all snow gear was left at the door on the beach towels—what a contrast, using beach towels for snow gear!

At one point, I gave Kayla and her friend who came over to help engineer the snowmen, the job of filling a mixing bowl with super clean snow so we could make snow cream. There were a few bits of nature in the bowl; but for the most part, each had a nice bowl of snow cream made with sugar, milk, vanilla, and a generous scoop of snow mixed together. I warned them not to eat it too quickly, which was completely unnecessary to warn twelve-year-olds of such a thing.

By the end of the day, the temperatures started to rise, and the two snowmen started to glaze over from the first layer of melt. The branch arms started to droop, and the walls of the snow fort seemed to shrink. Nevertheless, Kayla was in her element, on her knees, adding to the walls, making improvements to the snowmen, lying down in the snow, pitching snowballs at her brother and sister, thoroughly enjoying the snow day. She made the most of her time outside. Collin was picked up by a friend to spend the rest of the day and night. Kinsley was in and out on the back deck, with me being on high alert as to her whereabouts.

At the end of the day, my son Carl and his wife Erin came home after a wonderful getaway and exciting drive home in the snow. I left the little family, happy to be reunited since they are apart maybe once a year. They were happy to have a snow day, hot chocolate, grilled cheese sandwiches, and friends to share their excitement. I drove home, back to the mountains, confident that my new Michelin Defenders and my Subaru would get me there just fine. The snowplows had done their jobs, and the warmer temperatures made the drive safe. Beautiful fields of snow stretched out on either side of the road, and the old buildings and cottages of the mountains wore a blanket of white snow. The only road that was not plowed was my very own gravel road that led me to my house, which was waiting for me, affording me the contrast of an exciting day to a peaceful evening in front of the TV, under a warm fleece blanket.

Something Happens When You Start Getting Social Security

I was lying on the physical therapy table when I had to ask the therapist for the third time during our session, "How many repetitions and how many sets?"

He was very patient with me and told me the same answer as with the previous exercises, "Two sets of ten."

I replied, "Something happens to you when you start getting Social Security." I tend to make fun of myself to lighten the mood and to acknowledge that I know my attention span has shortened recently. The physical therapist seemed to appreciate my joke, or else he is well practiced in responding with a chuckle.

That got me to thinking about other things that I have noticed about being a retired person. I have new habits to streamline my life. For instance, I shed my bra at every opportunity but still have the sensitivity to wear one in public. If someone comes to the door unexpectedly, I have very close by, an overshirt with strategically placed pockets that I throw on over myself so I won't embarrass the visitor. So far, I have remembered to put it on before opening the door.

I do self-talk. For instance, when I lock the front door, I tell myself that I have locked the front door so that when I start the engine on my car, I won't get out of the car and double check. Then I need to remember that I told myself that I locked the door. So far, it seems to be working. I do the same when I park my car, telling myself, "I have parked near the cart corral and facing the left side of the store."

I am not too concerned that when I get up to do a task, start walking toward the room I plan to go to, arrive, then stop, and ask myself, "Now what was I going to do?" I usually remember after standing still for a moment or two. I suppose that if I don't remember, I could just forget about it. Oh, that's right, I did forget about it.

I think nothing of sleeping in the clothes I wore all day since all I ever wear are knits that stretch at every contact point. I'm not offending anyone, so I really don't care. In winter, I usually change my socks before crawling in bed. Don't worry, I do change my undergarment (down to one as I mentioned) regularly.

I make sure I have plenty of toilet paper on hand. I got tired of tracking down the kind of toilet paper I prefer, which is the Mega roll size. I know, I know, I will ultimately use the same amount of tissue no matter the size of the roll; but in my mind, changing out the roll every few days makes me feel like I am being shortchanged. I discovered the ability to subscribe to products on Amazon, so I have my twenty-four Mega rolls of Charmin Super Soft delivered every two months. This is one of my retirement-age indulgences.

Another is microwave dinners. They cost more, but they do taste better than my cooking. My cooking skills have slipped over the last five years since I haven't had to produce a square meal for anyone other than myself.

I have quit wearing lipstick. I cut my hair short, so it takes twenty seconds to spray with water and tousle it with my fingers. I have noticed that all the time I have saved by avoiding the makeup routine, I end up using it by putting lotion all over my body at least twice a day to rid myself of sandpaper skin. I can't get to the center of my back, so I have resorted to spreading lotion on the backside of a plastic mixing spoon to reach the unreachable parts of my back between my shoulder blades. I don't need the spoon anyway since I don't cook anymore, so it has its new home in my bathroom.

Now that I had a knee replacement and physical therapists are handling my right leg and knee, I do still shave my legs. I have discovered that an electric razor is a wonderful gadget that you can use while watching TV! When physical therapy is over, the electric shaver will find its home next to my old lipstick.

My TV watching has expanded from home improvement shows on HGTV to a fascination with British murder mysteries. I do have to put the captioning on since I have a hard time understanding the thick British accents. Thank goodness for the rewind button because my brain is not soaking in the plot, the characters, or the resolution to the crime.

I turn my TV on and then put it on pause immediately. That way, I can fast forward through the commercials, although I did find out that you need to pause the show for at least thirty minutes; or before you know it, you will be back to live TV. I have no patience for commercials anymore as if I have better things to do.

I drag myself off to bed around ten after watching perplexing British murder mysteries, only to wake up within a few hours to see through one squinting eye that the bedside

clock says 1:17 a.m. Then after a few more seemingly snooz-
ing moments, it says 3:54 a.m. And finally, when the clock
creeps as close to possible to 5:00 a.m., I throw the covers
off and start my morning routine. I have my first breakfast
and cup of tea, and since it is still dark outside, that breakfast really doesn't count since the sun has not shone through
the windows yet. I am ready for my second breakfast around
nine. By the second breakfast time, I have usually checked
my email, which by the way, is less and less, aired and made
the bed, started some kind of major housework, such as a
load of wash, run the vacuum cleaner, or gathered the trash,
mind you, not all in one day. The hummingbirds remind me
to check the feeder, and while I am outside, I whack down as
many cobwebs as I can find. All this has definitely earned a
second breakfast.

I do know why I wake frequently at night and get up so
early. It is because I snooze on the couch several times a day
only to wake up and wonder which house the couple chose
or who was the killer? Of course, as a young mom, I knew
how to get my baby on a sleep routine; but as an old mom,
I can't seem to remember how to do that for myself. I am
not aware of falling asleep. I sometimes wake up with a start
because I am having a coughing fit or startle myself awake
with a loud snort. I have actually found that sitting upright
in a chair instead of reclining on a couch makes no difference
at all. I still watch TV through closed eyelids.

I have a pair of reading glasses in each room of my
house, including the bathrooms. That prevents the eternal
hunt for a pair since I know that just inches or steps away
I will find some. Somehow, after a few days, they start to
disappear from the nearby end table or desktop, and I have
to round up the strays and start over again and spread them

back to their handy spots. Maybe I should do that self-talk and say, "I have taken my glasses off my head and put them back." Practice makes perfect.

Skating on Ice

U sing my phone, I took a snapshot of the tiny black-and-
white photo of the five of us, lined up in a row, by age
order, shod with skates, wrapped up in scarves and hats, pos-
ing on the frozen cranberry bog on which we took great joy
skating to our hearts' content. My sister requested this photo
to share with a friend who led a parallel childhood to ours.

I pushed the send button, then took my time to zoom
in the old photo, examining our faces, our clothing, the
background. This was sixty years ago when times were simple. The most complicated dilemma was finding enough dry
gear to wear outside during the winter months which offered
plentiful excitement from the simple natural elements created from freezing temperatures and precipitation.

Two days later, I found that, to my delight, my grand-
daughter wanted to celebrate her thirteenth birthday by
ice-skating at a temporary outdoor rink located in a shopping center. I was given a choice of participating or sitting
on the sidelines—in other words, "you don't have to skate if
you don't want to." Of course, I wanted to skate. Look at my
childhood, years of perfect balance on a single blade, skating
with ease, speed, and agility. No problem!

I visualized impressing my grandchildren with skilled ice-skating, holding hands as we sped by the beginner skaters, clutching the wall as they methodically navigated the ice on unfamiliar footgear. It was going to be great!

On the day of the ice-skating party, I planned my wardrobe. I needed to wear leggings under my jeans for warmth. I planned to wear a long-sleeved knit shirt under my itchy cashmere sweater, layered with a quilted vest, and a winter coat for good measure. A scarf, gloves, and two pairs of socks were needed for this winter night on the ice in Georgia.

When I arrived at the skating rink, the birthday girl and family were already zipping around the rink with the greatest of ease. I looked on as Kayla skated circles around everyone else. She made skating backward, spinning, even a few attempts at jumps, look easy. Oh my, she is a natural. I had no idea! Of course, her experience with in-line skating gave her the confidence and skills needed for ice-skating.

I proceeded to a nearby bench with my skates that I had retrieved from the skate hut. These were nothing like the white leather-laced skates I had as a young girl. They were uncomfortably rigid and clunky. But they had blades, hence qualified as ice skates. I tightened the fasteners to support my ankles. I rose to my feet and felt instantly tall and stately. The next goal was to get on the ice. That is when reality set in.

My blades hit the ice, and I felt precarious and frankly, in trouble. The waist high wall around the rink became my support as I held on to the rail and took short tentative steps, a few slippery slides, and made desperate attempts at finding my footing that would surely turn into the easy glides of ice-skating. This was embarrassing, and even more so, when four-year-old Kinsley made it a competition to see how quickly she could glide past her Oma. Her giggles were not lost on me. Her stability and sureness gave me no comfort regarding the pickle I had gotten myself into.

I would get the hang of it, perhaps after a few times around the rink, then ease myself away from the wall, but still within grasping distance. Each time around, I had the expectation that all the moving parts would come together, and I could glide along with poise and confidence. This never happened. I didn't understand why not. I finally decided to stay near the wall but advance to the next level by hovering my hand over the wall rail without holding on to it. Next thing I knew I was flat on the ice. In a flash, several people swarmed around me and all asked the same thing at the same time, "Are you all right?"

From my point of view, looking up from the ice, I saw pairs of clunky skates attached to legs, and worried faces attached to concerned voices. I had a mere moment to digest what just happened. I wanted to shout back, "I don't know if I'm all right yet. Give me a moment to figure it out!" Somehow, I managed to get back up by getting on my knees, pulling up on that traitorous wall, with the assistance of a couple of helping hands under my armpits. My vision of how I would create awe and admiration from my family was completely shattered! I would try again.

I went back to clutching the top of the wall, slowing down a bit, mustering up my courage to skate without any support as I approached one of two gaps in the wall that served as entrance/exit points. I unabashedly grabbed on to people, with permission of course, if they were standing in groups along the wall, blocking my single-minded path around the oval. I tried to stay cheerful and positive and even helped a young boy up and out of an icy water puddle.

Then out of nowhere, it happened again! I fell to the ice, severely hitting the side of my knee, and that darn swarm of concerned skaters magically appeared again. How was I going to live this down? I finally realized why there were so many concerned people ready to assist me. My gray hair! That automatically made me vulnerable, fragile, and a fall risk. Darn it! Dorothy Hamill, please show them, for me, the stuff we are made of.

In the end, I was relieved when our allotted time was up. I happily shed those skates, put on my comfy shoes, delivered the skates back to the skate shed, and said merry Christmas to the attendant. I secretly told myself that I did not need to ever skate again! Fortunately, I had not shared with my family that I had several years of skating experience sixty years ago. Those were the days. Let me cling to those times!

About the Author

❦

Marchiena Davis has been penning personal essays for many years to share with friends and family. Her upbringing in an immigrant Dutch family of seven has influenced her point of view to see everyday events in a humorous light. Marchiena graduated from Kennesaw State University with a degree in public and social services but later in life earned a degree in early childhood education. Her passion is to teach reading skills and confidence to struggling early readers. Living in Marietta, Georgia, she is a loving mom to three grown sons and Oma to seven delightful grandchildren.